Private
Pilot
Maneuvers

D1361168

JEPPESEN
SANDERSON

ii

Second Edition 1988
Third Edition 1989

JS314705C

© Jeppesen Sanderson, Inc., 1988, 1989
All Rights Reserved
55 Inverness Drive East, Englewood, CO 80112-5498
International Standard Book Number 0-88487-127-4

PREFACE ─────────────

The *Private Pilot Maneuvers Manual* is an authoritative operational guide for private pilot flight training. It is based on the "study/review" concept of learning. This means detailed material is presented in an uncomplicated way, then important points are summarized through the use of bold type and color. The manual incorporates many design features that will help you get the most out of your study and review efforts. These include:

● **Margin Notes** — The margin notes, which are printed in color, summarize key points from the text. You are encouraged to add your own study notes in the wide margins provided on each page.

● **Illustrations** — Illustrations are carefully planned to complement and expand upon concepts introduced in the text. Color in the illustrations and the accompanying captions flag them as items that warrant your attention during both initial study and review.

● **Bold Type** — Important new terms in the text are printed in bold type, then defined.

● **Checklist** — A checklist appears at the end of each section to help you verify your understanding of principal concepts.

● **Exercises** — An exercise section located in the back of the manual allows you to test yourself at the end of each section. An answer section follows the exercises.

The *Private Pilot Maneuvers Manual* is a flight training reference; you should study it during the same time period that you are learning new maneuvers and procedures in the airplane. You will find it beneficial to review previously studied areas throughout your training so that you will be thoroughly prepared for the practical test.

The sequence of subjects presented in the manual generally is designed around the chronological order that new maneuvers and procedures are introduced. Depending on the type of program you are enrolled in, it may be necessary to vary the sequence of study.

The *Private Pilot Maneuvers Manual,* in conjunction with the other private pilot course materials, will provide an effective, practical approach to your training. You may also note that the table of contents for your manual contains cross-references to video presentations. These video programs are available for your use at participating schools and are designed to enhance and complement your study. When used together, these various elements provide an ideal framework for you and your instructor as you prepare for the FAA written and practical tests.

TABLE OF CONTENTS

TEXT

EXERCISES

CHAPTER 1

GROUND OPERATIONS

INTRODUCTION

In this chapter, we introduce and explain some of the techniques and procedures you should follow during ground operations. These include preflight inspection, engine starting and shutdown, taxi operations, and tiedown procedures. Since these procedures can vary widely from airplane to airplane, the techniques presented in this chapter are intentionally general in nature. Be sure to consult the pilot's operating handbook for the procedures and checklists applicable to your airplane.

SECTION A

PREFLIGHT AND ENGINE STARTING

Safe flying begins on the ground. The attitudes and habits established in the initial stages of training greatly influence the standards you will follow throughout your flying career. Observe your instructor carefully as the preflight and engine-starting procedures are explained for the first time.

Perform the preflight inspection prior to each flight to ensure the aircraft is in a safe condition for the flight. As the pilot in command, you will be entirely responsible for making this decision. Any defects discovered during this inspection should be evaluated and, if required, corrected prior to that flight. Your flight instructor should point out the various components to be inspected and explain how to evaluate the airworthiness of an aircraft.

USE OF CHECKLISTS

Always use a written checklist to ensure all steps are completed.

Regardless of the number of times you repeat a procedure, follow a step-by-step checklist to ensure that all necessary items are accomplished in a logical sequence. Written checklists are used because of variations in types and models of airplanes and because it is unwise to rely on your memory.

PREFLIGHT INSPECTION

The preflight inspection is only the first of many procedures you will carry out according to a written checklist. The following discussion presents the proper sequence for a typical preflight inspection. [Figure 1-1]

In the cabin (position 1), check the aircraft papers to see that they consist of the following items:

1. Weight and balance data, including equipment list (required by FAA)
2. Radio station license (required by FCC)
3. Aircraft airworthiness certificate (required by FAA)
4. Aircraft registration certificate (required by FAA)
5. Engine and airframe logbooks (must be available, but not necessarily on board the aircraft)
6. Pilot's operating handbook or approved aircraft flight manual (required by FAA)

FAR Part 91 stipulates that an airplane must be operated in compliance with the operating limitations set forth in the approved flight manual. In

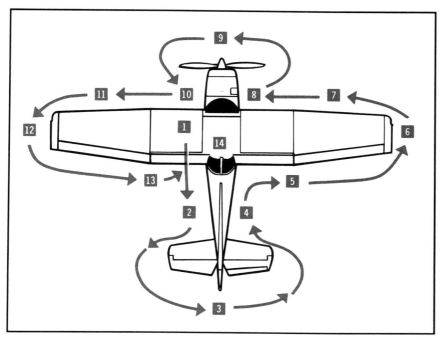

Figure 1-1. During the preflight inspection, you methodically check the airplane in a planned sequence. The steps for a typical airplane are outlined in the text with a numbered callout for each position.

addition to the required flight manual, often referred to as the pilot's operating handbook, specific placards and markings prescribed by the airworthiness standards for the particular airplane type must also be available.

Remove the control lock so the controls can be checked for freedom of movement. Then, as a safety precaution, make sure no one is standing near the propeller and turn the master switch ON. Next, check the fuel quantity gauges to ensure proper operation and to note the amount of fuel in each tank. Then, place the wing flaps in the full-down position, so you can examine the internal components, and turn the master switch OFF.

Next, check the windshield, or windscreen, and cabin windows for cleanliness and general condition. Inspect the instrument panel for any irregularities, such as cracked glass, and for any instruments or radios which have been removed for maintenance.

When all cabin checks are completed, verify that the magneto switch, master switch, mixture control, and throttle are in the appropriate OFF positions. Then, continue with the exterior part of the preflight check.

Inspect the left portion of the fuselage (position 2) for skin wrinkles, dents, and loose rivets. Examine the lower surface of the fuselage, which is especially susceptible to rock damage, for dents, cleanliness, and evidence of excessive engine oil leakage. If the static air source is located on the fuselage, examine it for obstructions. During cleaning or waxing of the airplane, the small static port can be plugged with wax. It is important that the static source be open so the airspeed, altimeter, and vertical speed indicators function properly.

You will need to inspect several items on the tail section (position 3). Remove the control surface lock, if installed, before you check the tail assembly. External locks are often used if gusty wind conditions are anticipated. Inspect the tail surfaces for general condition, looking closely for dents, skin wrinkles, and loose rivets. The underside and leading edge of the horizontal stabilizer (or stabilator) are easily damaged by rocks thrown up during takeoffs and landings on unimproved runway surfaces. Examine the elevator (or stabilator) and rudder for damage, loose hinge bolts, and freedom of movement. Inspect the control cables and stops for damage and the surface skin for dents and wrinkles. At this time, inspect the trim tab for security and general condition, the tail and beacon lights for damage, and the VOR navigation antenna. Finally, remove the tail tiedown chain or rope. If the airplane is equipped with a tailwheel, check the steering arms, cables, and springs for wear. In addition, inspect the tire for wear, proper inflation, cuts, and abrasions.

Go over the right portion of the fuselage (position 4), repeating the same procedures used at position 2. Next, inspect the right wing flap and aileron (position 5). Remove the control surface locks, if installed. Inspect the wing flap completely. Check the flap hinges for security, wear, and freedom of movement. Look over the aileron for security, damage, and freedom of movement. In addition, check the aileron pushrods or control cables for security, damage, and tension. Check the right wingtip (position 6) for damage and secure attachment. Then, inspect the right navigation light. Examine the leading edge of the right wing (position 7) for dents or other damage. Check the upper wing surface for frost or snow accumulation. Next, inspect the fuel tank vent opening and check the fuel drains, vents, and fuel quantity.

Check for fuel contamination before each flight.

Check the fuel tank drain for obstructions, security, and leakage. If the airplane is equipped with a quick-drain device, drain a few ounces of fuel into a clear container and examine it for the presence of water and other contaminants. You can detect water, because it is heavier than avgas and settles to the bottom of the container. It contrasts clearly with the color of the avgas. Since fuel contamination is possible at any time, you should do this check before every flight.

Inspect the fuel quantity level by removing the filler cap and looking into the tank. The quantity in the tank should agree with the fuel gauge reading you observed on the associated fuel gauge. After you have checked the fuel level, replace the filler cap and tighten it securely. Finally, remove the tiedown chain or rope.

Inspect the attachment points of the main landing gear (position 8) for dents and wrinkles. Check the tire for wear, cuts, abrasions, and proper inflation. Inspect the wheel fairing, if installed, for cracks, dents, and general security. Look at the hydraulic brake and brake lines for security and leaks. Give particular attention to proper inflation of the gear strut.

Check the front cowl openings (position 9) for obstructions. Inspect the engine compartment, which is accessible through the cowl access door, for loose wires and clamps, worn hoses, and oil or fuel leaks. Determine the oil quantity by removing and reading the dipstick. Add oil if the level is below the minimum recommended by the manufacturer. Then, replace the dipstick, tighten it securely, and check the oil filler cap for security. Drain the fuel strainer (if located within the engine compartment) for several seconds to eliminate any water or other contaminants that may have collected in it. Water can form in the fuel tanks from condensation of moisture in the air, or it may be present in fuel added to the tanks. Finally, close the access door.

The cowl flaps, if installed, should be checked for security. Then, inspect the propeller and spinner, and check the propeller blades and tips for nicks and scratches. Propeller nicks can cause excessive stress in the metal of the propeller. They should be repaired by a certificated mechanic prior to flight. If your airplane has a constant-speed propeller, check it for oil leakage. You can generally detect leakage by the presence of oil streaks along the backsides of the propeller blades. In cold weather, you should carefully pull the propeller through two or three revolutions in the direction of normal propeller rotation. This procedure loosens the congealed oil and makes engine starting easier.

Check the windshield and cabin windows (position 10) for cleanliness and general condition. Do not use a dry rag to clean the windshield, because it can scratch the surface. Only a cloth and cleaning compound specifically designed for airplane windshields should be used.

Check the communications antenna for general condition and security. Use the same procedure to check the left main landing gear as was used at position 8.

Inspect the left wing structure (position 11) in the same manner you used on the right wing. Then, remove the tiedown chain or rope. Next, inspect the fuel tank vent opening. Perform the checks of the fuel tank drains, vents, and fuel quantity in the same manner described in position 7.

Remove the pitot tube cover, if installed, and check the tube opening for obstructions. A plugged pitot tube opening causes the airspeed indicator to malfunction. In addition, the pitot tube itself should show no signs of damage and should not be bent out of alignment. Also, be sure to check the static port if it is located on the pitot tube. Check the stall warning vane on the leading edge of the wing for freedom of movement. It is a good practice to turn on the master switch just prior to the stall warning vane inspection. This enables you to check the stall warning signal when the vane is deflected upward. Remember to turn the master switch OFF immediately after making this inspection. If your airplane is equipped with a pneumatic stall warning device, check the leading edge opening for obstructions.

Examine the left wingtip (position 12), using the same procedure you used for the right. Inspect the left wing flap and aileron (position 13), using the same steps that were used for the right. After loading the baggage, close the door and make sure it is secure (position 14).

STARTING PROCEDURES

After you have completed the preflight inspection, you are ready to begin the prestarting checklist. Since there are a number of different procedures used to start airplane engines, it is important to use an appropriate written checklist. [Figure 1-2]

Although the starting procedure can vary from airplane to airplane, there are certain common safety precautions and suggestions that apply universally. You should avoid starting the engine with the tail of the airplane pointed toward parked automobiles, spectators, or an open hangar. In addition to being discourteous, wind blast and debris could injure persons and damage property.

STARTING THE ENGINE

1. Carburetor heat — COLD
2. Mixture — RICH
3. Primer — AS REQUIRED (up to 6 strokes, none if engine is warm)
4. Throttle — OPEN ½ INCH (CLOSED if engine is warm)
5. Propeller area — CLEAR
6. Master switch — ON
7. Ignition switch — START (release when engine starts)
8. Oil pressure — CHECK (30 seconds summer, 60 seconds winter)

Figure 1-2. This checklist is typical for a single-engine airplane. Follow the recommendations of the airplane manufacturer for the best engine-starting method.

If you are using an unimproved surface, inspect the ground under the propeller before you start the engine. Rocks, pebbles, or any other loose debris can be picked up by the propeller and hurled backward. Remove any such particles to avoid damaging the propeller and other parts of the airplane. If this is not possible, move the airplane to another location before you start the engine.

The following discussion is based on a typical starting sequence for a training airplane. Always use a checklist appropriate to the airplane you are flying. [Figure 1-3]

Place the carburetor heat control (item 1) in the COLD position. When the control is placed in this position, the air entering the engine is filtered to remove dust and dirt. Next, set the mixture control (item 2) to RICH, then use the primer (item 3) to pump fuel into the engine cylinders. This will help you to start the engine in cold weather. The number of primer strokes required depends on the length of time the engine has been shut down and the temperature of the outside air. If the engine has been shut down for less than an hour or it is a warm day, it probably will start without priming. Most light airplane operator's handbooks recommend that you use from two to six strokes of the engine primer. Colder

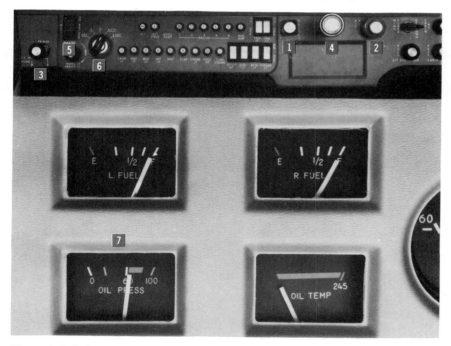

Figure 1-3. Before you begin the starting sequence, make sure you are familiar with the location and operation of each of the controls. The numbered callouts in the art correspond to the items referenced in the text.

temperatures require the greater number of strokes. Open the throttle (item 4) one-half inch so that when the engine starts it is operating at a low speed which lessens engine wear.

Always clear the area, both verbally and visually, before starting the engine.

Now, clear the area. To do this, you should open a window or door, look for anyone in the area, then shout, "Clear!" to warn anyone near the airplane that the propeller is about to rotate. You should then listen for a reply to ensure that there is no one in the immediate area. When you are sure that the area is clear, turn the master switch ON (item 5) to supply electrical power to the ignition switch. Then, rotate or press the ignition switch to supply power to the starter motor (item 6). When the engine starts, return the switch to the BOTH position. It is important to release the starter as soon as the engine starts to avoid damage to the starter motor.

Check the oil pressure immediately after starting the engine.

After the engine is running smoothly, adjust the throttle to a low power setting. This prevents undue friction within the engine before the lubricating oil has had a chance to coat the engine's internal parts thoroughly. It is important to check immediately that the oil pressure gauge is in the green arc (item 7). If the oil pressure does not register properly within 30 seconds in warm weather or 60 seconds in cold weather, shut down the engine. This will prevent possible damage and will allow you to determine the nature of the problem.

CHECKLIST ━━━━━━━━━━━━━━━━━━━━━

After studying this section, you should have a basic understanding of:

✓ **Checklist** — The importance of written checklists.

✓ **Preflight** — The purpose of a preflight inspection, including a general understanding of what items are checked and why.

✓ **Starting** — Procedures used in starting an airplane, including general safety procedures.

TAXIING, ENGINE SHUTDOWN, AND TIEDOWN

In this section, you are introduced to some of the techniques and procedures used during taxi operations. Next, you will learn procedures and cautions for engine shutdown and for securing the airplane.

TAXIING

You usually begin learning about taxiing on the first training flight. During taxi practice, you learn directional control techniques and proper throttle usage. Later in the training program, you will learn which control positions to use during crosswind takeoffs and landings. Airplanes which have tricycle landing gear and steerable nosewheels are relatively easy to taxi. However, there are techniques which you must learn, and some precautions that you should observe.

USE OF THE THROTTLE

In general, good throttle use is based on smooth, precise adjustments of power. Erratic throttle movement can cause directional control difficulties. To help you make proper adjustments, a friction adjustment is incorporated in the throttle assembly. [Figure 1-4]

Correct taxi techniques require correct power control. For example, more power is required to start the airplane moving than to keep it moving. You should add power slowly until the airplane starts rolling, then reduce it. You also will find that you need a greater amount of power to start and sustain an airplane in motion on a soft surface than on a hard surface.

Figure 1-4. The friction control adjusts the throttle's resistance to movement, so your natural arm movements do not overcontrol the throttle. In addition, the friction adjustment prevents the throttle from moving because of engine vibration.

Control taxi speed with the throttle, and use the brakes only when needed.

Control taxi speed primarily with the throttle and secondarily with the brakes. Use the brakes only when a reduction of engine r.p.m. is not sufficient to slow the airplane. Using the brakes to control the airplane's speed causes excessive wear and overheating of the braking system. Light airplanes usually have brakes on only two wheels, and the brakes are relatively small. For this and other reasons, many flight instructors recommend operating at a taxi speed that is no faster than a brisk walk. When you are operating in confined areas, however, keep your speed slow enough to allow you to stop safely without using the brakes. You should be able to stop by reducing power or by shutting down the engine. A useful suggestion for developing proper taxi speed control is for you to assume that the brakes are inoperative. This will help you learn proper use of power to control taxi speed.

ENGINE COOLING DURING TAXIING

Many air-cooled engines are tightly enclosed by the cowling. Because of the slow speeds associated with taxiing and ground operations, only small amounts of cooling air flow into the engine compartment and over the engine cylinders. Prolonged ground operations, particularly in warm weather, can cause overheating in the engine cylinders even before the oil temperature gauge indicates a pronounced rise in temperature. If your airplane has a cylinder head temperature gauge, use it to monitor engine temperature. You should refer to the airplane's POH for the recommended power settings for engine warmup to provide the optimum flow of cooling air through the engine compartment.

DIRECTIONAL CONTROL DURING TAXI

During ground operations, you normally depress the left rudder pedal to turn left and the right pedal to turn right.

On most airplanes, the nosewheel is linked to the rudder pedals, and you steer during taxi operations by using rudder pressure. When you depress the right rudder pedal, the nosewheel turns to the right, causing the airplane to turn right. If you depress the left rudder pedal, the nosewheel turns to the left, causing the airplane to turn left. The amount that you can turn the nosewheel varies with different makes and models of airplanes.

To make tight turns, apply full rudder pressure, then apply the brake on that rudder pedal.

In addition to turning the nosewheel in the direction of the turn, depressing the rudder pedal also causes the rudder to move. Therefore, airflow over the rudder from propeller slipstream may provide a small additional force which assists you in turning the airplane. To make a turn of a smaller radius than you can accomplish through nosewheel steering alone, depress the rudder pedal fully in the direction of the turn, then lightly apply the individual toe brake on that rudder pedal. This procedure applies braking in the direction of the turn and produces a smaller turn radius.

EFFECTS OF WIND ON TAXI TECHNIQUES

The basic skills just discussed allow you to taxi effectively in calm or light wind conditions. However, when wind speed is moderate or strong, you must use special techniques. In a strong wind, there is a tendency for the wind to get under the upwind wing and tip the airplane toward the downwind side. You can counteract this tendency by using the flight controls properly. The aileron, rudder, and elevator (or stabilator) controls are relatively ineffective at slow speeds. However, as the speed of air over the controls increases, control effectiveness also increases. The flight controls respond the same, whether you are taxiing at five knots with no wind or sitting still with a five-knot headwind. However, if you taxi the airplane at 15 knots into a 15-knot wind, the controls have a 30-knot airflow over them and respond to that velocity of airflow.

On the other hand, if you taxi the airplane at five knots with a tailwind of five knots, the taxi speed and the wind speed are canceled, and the controls respond as though no wind exists. If you slow the airplane, the controls respond as though there were an increasing tailwind component. When you stop the airplane completely, the control surfaces are subjected to the direct effects of a five-knot tailwind.

TAXIING IN HEADWINDS

When you taxi an airplane directly into a headwind, the wind flows over and under both wings equally and has no tendency to tip the airplane. Under these conditions, you should hold the elevator (or stabilator) control near neutral, or slightly forward of neutral, to exert normal pressure on the nose gear.

If you hold the control wheel full forward in a strong headwind, the wind striking the downward deflection of the elevator (or stabilator) forces the tail section up and the nose down. This condition places more than the normal weight on the nose gear, compresses the nose strut, and brings the propeller tips closer to the ground. Normally, this is not hazardous. On rough terrain, however, this procedure can cause the propeller to be damaged by contact with the ground. [Figure 1-5]

Figure 1-5. When taxiing over rough ground into a strong headwind, you should hold back the control wheel so the elevator (or stabilator) is raised. This procedure forces the tail down and increases propeller clearance.

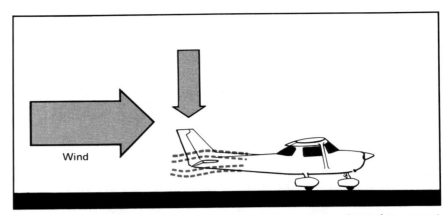

Figure 1-6. With a tailwind, full forward control wheel pressure is used to prevent the wind from raising the tail and causing the airplane to nose over.

TAXIING IN TAILWINDS

When you are taxiing in a strong tailwind, place the control wheel in the full-forward position. This causes the wind to strike the upper surface of the elevator (or stabilator) and to exert a downward force on the tail. [Figure 1-6]

TAXIING IN CROSSWINDS

Crosswinds cause a lifting effect on one wing. Normally, the wind is not strong enough to actually overturn the airplane. With a strong wind and improper control placement, though, the airplane could be upset, resulting in serious damage.

QUARTERING HEADWIND

To counteract the tipping tendencies of a left quartering headwind, apply neutral elevator (or stabilator) pressure and turn the control wheel full left. Then, the wind flowing over the left wing exerts pressure against the raised aileron, tending to force that wing down. Be sure to move the aileron control to its full deflection. The controls are less effective at slow taxi speeds, and a small amount of deflection may be of little value. [Figure 1-7]

With a quartering headwind from the right, the tipping tendency is to the left. Therefore, right aileron is required. [Figure 1-8]

Taxiing with a quartering headwind is similar to the conditions you encounter in a crosswind takeoff or landing. Your understanding of the effects of wind on taxiing will help you develop your crosswind takeoff and landing techniques.

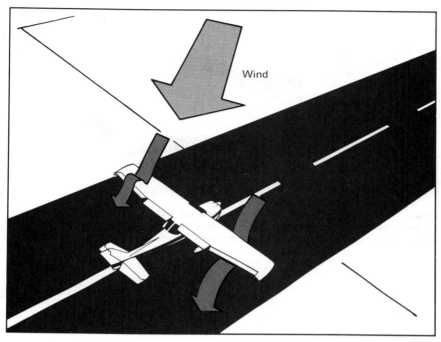

Figure 1-7. As wind velocity increases, the tipping tendency becomes more pronounced. However, with a strong wind, the ailerons are more effective and tend to compensate for this effect.

QUARTERING TAILWIND

When the wind is striking the airplane from behind, you must position the ailerons to counteract the tipping tendency and rotate the control wheel away from the wind. When the wind is from the left rear (a left

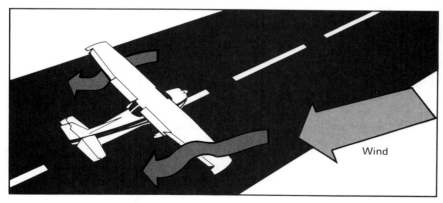

Figure 1-8. In a right quartering headwind, apply neutral elevator (or stabilator) and turn the control wheel full right to raise the right aileron and lower the left aileron.

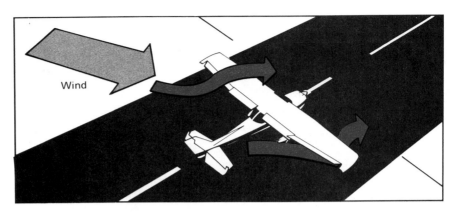

Figure 1-9. A left quartering tailwind requires full right aileron deflection and full forward elevator (or stabilator) pressure. In a right quartering tailwind, full left aileron deflection and full forward elevator (or stabilator) is used.

quartering tailwind), turn the aileron control to the right. Since quartering tailwinds also have a tendency to flow beneath the elevator (or stabilator) and lift the tail, the airplane may tip over on the nosewheel and one main wheel. To counteract this tipping force, move the control wheel full forward to lower the elevator (or stabilator). The tailwind then applies an aerodynamic force on the top of the elevator (or stabilator) and tends to push the tail down. [Figure 1-9]

Use extra care when slowing down or turning in a quartering tailwind.

You must be particularly cautious when you are slowing down and beginning a turn in a quartering tailwind. The increasing tailwind component, combined with the normal tendency of the airplane to tip during the turn, makes the airplane especially vulnerable to being overturned. Slow taxi speeds and slow turns minimize this danger.

PRACTICING PROPER CONTROL POSITIONING

While taxiing, you should practice proper control wheel placement.

During much of the time that you spend taxiing, the winds probably will be at a level where control positioning is not critical. However, proper control placement requires practice. Therefore, you should practice proper control positioning on every flight. When there are light winds, assume that the winds are strong and from whichever direction the windsock indicates. In this way, you can practice correct placement of the aileron and elevator (or stabilator) controls as if it were necessary.

The benefits of this practice will be evident later in the flight training program when you actually encounter strong winds. In addition, you will develop a constant awareness of wind direction early in the program. By the time you reach the takeoff position on any given flight, you already will have evaluated wind speed and direction.

Figure 1-10. Some of the more common hand signals are shown here. You should review them periodically, especially during the early portion of your flight training program.

HAND SIGNALS

You should be familiar with the standard hand signals used by ramp personnel for directing you during ground operations. However, keep in mind that, even when you are being directed, you continue to be responsible for the safe operation of your airplane. [Figure 1-10]

As pilot in command, you are always responsible for the safe operation of your airplane.

ENGINE SHUTDOWN AND PARKING PROCEDURES

At the completion of a flight, taxi the airplane into the parking area, using a safe taxi speed and proper control procedures. After you reach the desired parking area, you may wish to check for accidental activation of the ELT by tuning 121.5 MHz just before you shut down the radios. This helps eliminate false ELT alarms and preserves the ELT's batteries until they may be needed. Then, proceed with the engine shutdown according to the appropriate checklist. As an extra precaution, make sure you remove the key from the ignition.

MOVING THE AIRPLANE

You can safely and easily maneuver most light tricycle-gear airplanes by using a towbar attached to the nosewheel. The towbar normally is stowed in the baggage compartment and should be used when available.

Fixed-base operators usually have an assortment of towbars for use if you do not have one in the airplane. When you use a towbar, be sure the nose gear is not turned beyond its steering radius limits.

MOVING THE AIRPLANE WITHOUT A TOWBAR

Since an airplane is composed of lightweight materials, only certain points may be used for pushing or pulling it. Your instructor will show you the location of bulkheads and ribs located under the skin of the airplane. Normally, these are the points you will use when a towbar is not available.

PIVOTING THE AIRPLANE

You can pivot a tricycle-gear airplane if the nose gear is lifted off the ground. Apply downward pressure on the tail section. With the tail depressed, the nosewheel will clear the ground, allowing you to turn the airplane readily in either direction. [Figure 1-11]

Observe the wingtips of the airplane carefully, since one wingtip moves aft while the other one moves forward. Structural damage can result if a wingtip strikes another object.

It is easy to pivot a tailwheel-type airplane, because the tailwheel usually pivots 360°. One person can turn the airplane around by pushing on the side of the fuselage over a bulkhead.

PUSHING THE AIRPLANE

Pushing on the leading edge of the horizontal and vertical stabilizers is acceptable if you are cautious. Apply pressure only to the leading edge near the fuselage.

Figure 1-11. You can apply downward pressure on the tail by pushing on the fuselage directly over a bulkhead (A) and/or by pushing down on the front spar of the horizontal stabilizer adjacent to the fuselage (B).

The leading edge of the wing is also a good push point on low-wing airplanes. Apply pressure only at rib locations. When the wing is used as a push point, more than one person is needed to maintain directional control of the airplane. On high-wing airplanes, wing struts make good push points.

You can also push or pull the airplane by its propeller. However, only apply pressure near the propeller hub. If you apply pressure to the propeller tip, it may be permanently bent and produce a serious vibration problem in flight. The nosecap, engine cowling, and the trailing edges of wings and control surfaces are not designed for moving the airplane, and you should not use them for this purpose.

SECURING THE AIRPLANE

Proper tiedown procedures are the best precaution against damage to a parked airplane from strong or gusty winds. When the airplane is in the proper tiedown area, place chocks in front of and behind the main wheels and release the parking brake (if set).

Secure all flight controls to prevent the control surfaces from striking their stops. Most airplanes are equipped with internal control locks. Others may require you to use external padded battens (control surface locks). Even if the airplane is equipped with internal control locks, it may be necessary to use external locks to prevent gust loads from being fed back into the control system during extremely strong or gusty wind conditions. When you use external control locks, you should fasten streamers or tiedown lines to the locks. This alerts you and airport ramp personnel to remove the external locks prior to flight.

Before you leave the airplane, secure it with tiedown ropes or chains. Secure the tiedowns without slack, but not tight. Too much slack allows the airplane to jerk against the ropes or chains, while too little slack may permit high stresses to be placed on the airplane. The tail tiedown should be secure, but not so tight that it raises the nose of the airplane. In a headwind, a raised nose increases the angle of attack of the wing and creates additional lifting force, causing more pressure on the wing tiedown restraints.

CLEANUP

After the airplane is secured, you should make a careful check of the interior of the airplane. Make sure all switches are off and that trash, papers, and flight planning items are cleaned from the cabin area. On the exterior of the airplane, install the pitot tube cover, if applicable. Place the propeller in a horizontal position to lessen the possibility of damage to another taxiing aircraft's wingtip. Placing the propeller in a horizontal position also permits the spinner to offer more protection to the prop hub from rain, snow, and ice. This is especially important if an aircraft is equipped with a constant-speed propeller.

CHECKLIST _____

After studying this section, you should have a basic understanding of:

✓ **Taxiing** — The procedures and proper control placements to use when taxiing an airplane in various wind conditions, including headwinds, tailwinds, crosswinds, and quartering tailwinds.

✓ **Hand signals** — Some of the more common hand signals used by ground personnel to direct airplanes while taxiing.

✓ **Shutdown** — Procedures to follow when shutting down the airplane, including checking for activation of the airplane's ELT.

✓ **Moving the airplane** — How to move the airplane by hand without damaging the skin or internal components of the airframe.

✓ **Securing the airplane** — How airplane controls are secured and how to tie down the airplane to the ramp by the use of chains or ropes.

PRIMARY MANEUVERS

CHAPTER 2

INTRODUCTION

The first step in mastering the skill of flying is learning the fundamentals: straight-and-level flight, climbs, descents, and turns. All other flight maneuvers and procedures are combinations of these four basics. Progress through your flight training program will depend on your mastery of these techniques.

Another important skill learned early in flight training is collision avoidance. You accomplish this by continuously searching for other aircraft and applying right-of-way rules when you spot one. During your training, your instructor will remind you to continually watch for other aircraft and will introduce clearing turns and scanning techniques at the appropriate times.

SECTION A

STRAIGHT-AND-LEVEL FLIGHT

Your flight training will normally begin with instruction in the techniques of straight-and-level flight. The objectives of this maneuver are to point the airplane in a particular direction, maintain that direction, and fly at a predetermined altitude.

LEVEL FLIGHT

For a given power setting, there is a fixed nose and wing position which result in level flight.

You control the airplane's direction and altitude by controlling the nose and wing positions with reference to the natural horizon. This is called **attitude flying**. During training in attitude flying, you learn that there is a fixed nose position (pitch attitude) and a fixed wing position (bank attitude) for each flight condition. With a constant power setting and the aircraft's attitude adjusted to these fixed positions, the aircraft will maintain the selected flight conditions.

You should be aware of the difference between visual flying and instrument flying. **Visual flying** simply means that the natural horizon is used as a reference point. **Instrument flying** requires you to use the flight instruments for airplane attitude reference. The attitude indicator, altimeter, and the heading indicator give you most of the information you need to maintain straight-and-level flight. [Figure 2-1]

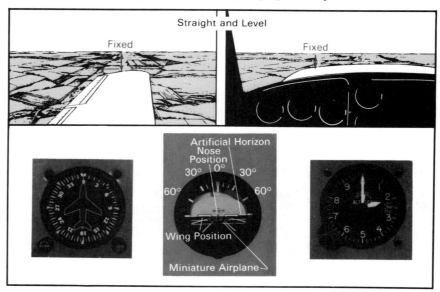

Figure 2-1. The visual and instrument presentations shown here are representative of what you will see when the airplane is established in straight-and-level flight.

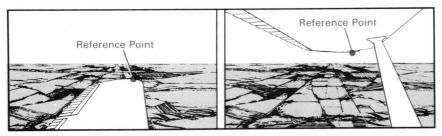

Figure 2-2. As you look out the left window of the cockpit, this is how the level flight attitude appears in a low-wing or high-wing airplane.

CONTROLLING BANK ATTITUDE

In straight-and-level flight, the wings remain level with the horizon, and the flight path is parallel to the earth's surface. To maintain this configuration, it is necessary to fix the relationship of the airplane to the horizon. To do this, pick a point on the wingtip for a reference; the wings-level position is maintained by keeping the wingtips a given distance above or below the horizon. [Figure 2-2]

CONTROLLING PITCH ATTITUDE

To control pitch attitude, or nose position, select a point on the airplane's nose or a spot on the windshield as a reference point. This point should be directly in front of you. [Figure 2-3]

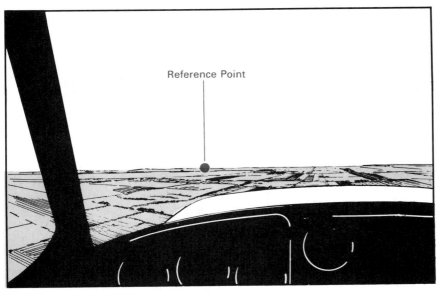

Figure 2-3. When viewed from the pilot's seat, this is how straight-and-level flight will appear.

The exact appearance of the wingtips and nose in reference to the horizon depends on the type of airplane being flown, your height, and how you position your seat. A key element in attitude flying is determining the wing and nose positions that result in level flight.

CONTROLLING HEADING AND ALTITUDE

Cross-check the flight instruments to verify heading and altitude.

In practicing straight-and-level flight, you learn to maintain a specific heading and altitude by establishing the wing and nose attitudes for level flight. Then, you periodically refer to the heading indicator and altimeter to verify that you are on the desired heading and at the preselected altitude.

ATTITUDE FLYING

To fly by instrument reference, you will need to learn the techniques of scanning. Develop the habit of keeping your eyes moving continuously between outside reference points and the instruments, always remaining alert for other air traffic in your vicinity. At no time should you concentrate entirely on any one reference. [Figure 2-4]

Several forces may cause the airplane to drift from the desired attitude. Power changes, turbulence, wind gusts, and brief periods of inattention to wing position can all cause changes in heading or altitude.

When you notice a variation from the selected heading or altitude, first reestablish straight-and-level flight, then apply necessary corrections.

Since flying is a continuous series of small adjustments, you must learn to maintain a desired attitude as closely as possible and make smooth, prompt corrections as necessary. Abrupt changes can result in over-correcting. Each correction should be made in two steps. First, if the heading or altitude has changed, apply control pressure to return to a straight-and-level flight attitude. Second, adjust the attitude reference points to return the airplane slowly to the desired heading and altitude, and adjust the power setting, if required. The nose position helps you to

Figure 2-4. Your eyes should move from one wing to the nose, to the appropriate instruments, and then to the other wing.

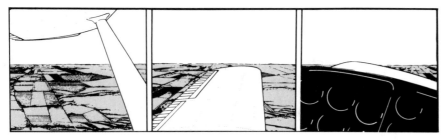

Figure 2-5. Here is an example of an airplane in a nose-high right bank. The left wing and nose are above their normal straight-and-level positions. Notice also how the wing is inclined to the horizon, indicating a nose-high attitude.

know when the wings are not level. The position of the wingtip also provides a small clue when the nose is high or low. [Figure 2-5]

ATTITUDE AND ELEVATOR MOVEMENT

Changes in pitch attitude, caused by movement of the elevator (or stabilator), result in altitude changes during cruising flight. The elevator (or stabilator) also affects the rate of climb or descent during altitude changes. Since it controls the pitch position of the nose, we can say that altitude is controlled primarily by the elevator (or stabilator) in straight-and-level flight.

AIRSPEED AND POWER

After you gain reasonable control over the airplane attitude, you will be able to control airspeed primarily with power. The throttle is used mainly to control airspeed and the elevator (or stabilator) to control altitude. After cruise airspeed has been established and power is constant, it is possible to use airspeed variations to detect pitch attitude changes. [Figure 2-6]

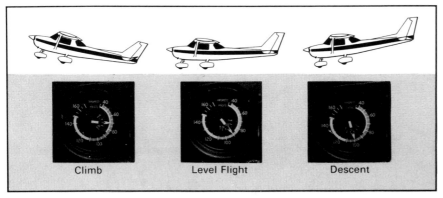

Figure 2-6. If power remains constant, any change in pitch will be reflected as an increase or decrease in airspeed.

TRIM

Trim adjustments eliminate the need for continuous forward or backward pressure on the wheel to maintain attitude. If the airplane feels nose-heavy, you are holding back pressure to maintain a given attitude. Likewise, if forward pressure is required, the airplane will feel tail-heavy. When it is properly trimmed, you will not have to apply either forward or back pressure to maintain a constant pitch attitude. [Figure 2-7]

Use the trim to relieve control wheel pressure.

Use the trim tab only to remove control wheel pressure; do not use it to fly the airplane. The proper procedure is to set the airplane in the desired pitch attitude and at the selected airspeed, then trim away any control pressure necessary to hold that attitude. With a few exceptions, trim tab adjustments should be made whenever you must apply a continuous forward or rearward force to the control wheel.

EFFECTS OF RUDDER USE

Airplanes are designed to remain in stable, aerodynamic balance during cruising flight. Therefore, aileron or rudder pressures are not constantly required. This balanced condition is sometimes referred to as flying "hands off," meaning that you can remove your hands and feet from the controls and the airplane will continue to maintain straight-and-level flight.

During normal flight, the rudder is streamlined with the airflow over the airplane. The ball of the turn coordinator should remain in the center of

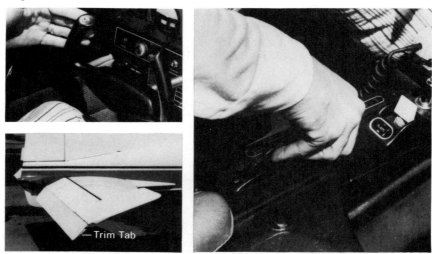

Figure 2-7. In this example, back pressure is being applied to maintain a constant pitch attitude (top left). By rotating the trim wheel in the nose-up direction (right), the trim tab will move down (bottom left) and deflect air passing over the elevator, causing a reduction in required back pressure. Rotate the trim wheel until all pressure is eliminated.

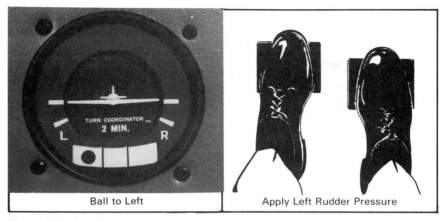

Figure 2-8. A rule you can use for rudder correction is, "When the ball is out of center, step on the ball." Here the ball is to the left of center, and you must apply left rudder pressure to center it.

the inclinometer. If the ball moves out of the center when you are maneuvering, the airplane is skidding or slipping. Apply rudder pressure to return the ball to the center. [Figure 2-8]

STRAIGHT-AND-LEVEL FLIGHT BY INSTRUMENT REFERENCE

After practicing straight-and-level flight using visual references, your instructor will have you repeat this practice using only instrument references. You will find that the airplane responds just as it does when it is flown visually. During flight by instruments, the attitude indicator is your primary flight instrument, since it is the only instrument that displays both pitch and bank information. [Figure 2-9]

 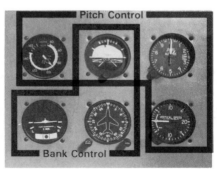

Figure 2-9. As shown on the left, a typical instrument panel is arranged in what is called the basic "T" configuration. In this arrangement, the attitude indicator is at the center of the "T," and supporting instruments are beside and below it. On the right, you can see that the attitude, airspeed, and vertical speed indicators, as well as the altimeter, are used to control the pitch attitude of the airplane. Bank is controlled by use of the attitude indicator, heading indicator, and turn coordinator.

Deviation from desired altitudes and headings is caused by the same forces, whether you are flying by instrument references or visual references. Corrections also are made in the same way. When the bank attitude and heading have changed, or are changing, first return to a straight-and-level flight attitude. Next, look at the altimeter and heading indicator to determine the amount of correction needed to return to the original altitude and heading. Finally, make small attitude corrections to return to the desired altitude and heading.

KINESTHETIC SENSE

Kinesthetic sense is generally defined as the feel of motion and pressure changes through nerve endings in the organs, muscles, and tendons. This is the feeling pilots describe as the "seat of the pants" sensation. If you rely solely on this sense when flying by instrument references, it is possible to experience **spatial disorientation.** This is an incorrect mental image of your position, attitude, or movement in relation to what is actually happening to your airplane. It can cause an inexperienced pilot to make incorrect control movements. Therefore, during instrument flight, it is extremely important to believe only what your instruments tell you and not respond to your physical sensations.

CHECKLIST _____

After studying this section, you should have a basic understanding of:

✓ **Straight-and-level flight** — How to establish and maintain straight-and-level flight using visual references.

✓ **Attitude flying** — What scanning is, how to apply it, and the differences between visual and instrument flying.

✓ **Maintaining heading and altitude** — What the procedures are for correcting deviations in heading and altitude.

CLIMBS AND DESCENTS

In Section A, the objective was to maintain altitude. In this section, you will learn how to change altitude by precisely controlling airplane pitch and power. When practicing climbs, your objectives are to become proficient in establishing the proper climb attitude, to apply the appropriate control pressures, and to trim the airplane correctly to maintain the climb attitude. During practice climbs, it is important to learn the relationships between attitude and power, as well as between climb speed and climb performance.

CLIMBS

Enter a climb by adding power smoothly to establish the recommended climb power setting and increasing back pressure on the control wheel. The back pressure raises the nose of the airplane smoothly until the desired climb attitude is established. [Figure 2-10]

A climb is established by adjusting both pitch and power.

As the climb attitude is established, the airspeed gradually slows and stabilizes on or near the desired climb speed. The combination of the climb attitude and the climb power setting determines the airplane's performance.

The airspeed indicator provides an indirect indication of pitch attitude. If you see that the airspeed is lower than you desire, use the pitch attitude references to lower the airplane's nose position. Conversely, if the airspeed is higher than you desire, you must raise the airplane's nose position. Then, retrim slightly when the new attitude produces the desired climb speed. Use the position of the wingtips and the angle which they

Figure 2-10. The climb attitude represented by the nose position and the attitude indicator should resemble these.

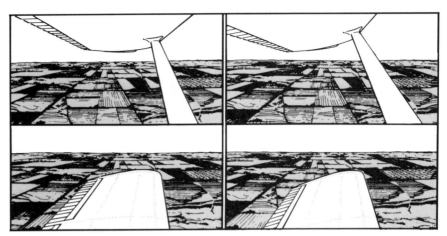

Figure 2-11. The left side shows the left wingtip as it appears when the airplane is flying level for both high- and low-wing airplanes. The right side shows the same wingtip when the airplane is in a climb attitude.

make with the horizon to establish the proper climb attitude, just as you used them to establish level flight attitudes. [Figure 2-11]

LEFT-TURNING TENDENCY DURING THE CLIMB

Right rudder pressure is required during a climb.

As the airplane climbs, it tends to turn to the left, and the ball of the turn coordinator tends to move off center to the right. Use right rudder pressure to maintain coordination and return the ball to the center of the inclinometer. A combination of forces such as P-factor, torque, and spiraling slipstream causes this left-turning tendency. The effects are most pronounced at high power settings and low airspeeds, such as those used during climbs.

Manufacturers design airplanes to compensate for the left-turning tendency during cruising flight. However, at other power settings or speeds, you must apply rudder pressure to counteract this tendency. Rudder trim tabs are used to counteract the left-turning tendency on more powerful airplanes.

MAINTAINING THE CLIMB

Refer to the airspeed indicator, altimeter, and the ball of the turn coordinator to monitor the climb. If changes are necessary, make small adjustments after looking at the nose and wingtip positions or the attitude indicator. Then, allow the airplane to stabilize in the new attitude and remove control pressures by trimming.

CLIMB SPEEDS

Early in your flight training, your instructor will introduce you to several specific climb speeds. Each of these speeds has a difference effect on the airplane's climb performance and, therefore, is used at different times.

The **best rate-of-climb** speed is an important performance speed. It provides the most gain in altitude in the least amount of time. The **best angle-of-climb** speed results in a steeper climb. It is used to clear obstacles in the takeoff path, such as trees or powerlines at the end of the runway. It is generally the slowest of the specified climb speeds. [Figure 2-12]

Use **cruise climb speed** to achieve a higher groundspeed while climbing to cruising altitude during cross-country flight. This speed usually is higher than the other climb speeds and provides better engine cooling. It also improves forward visibility over the nose of the airplane. You can determine the cruise climb speed, as well as the best rate-of-climb and angle-of-climb speeds, by referring to the pilot's operating handbook.

LEVELOFF FROM A CLIMB

To return to straight-and-level flight from a climb, begin the transition before you reach the desired altitude. The amount of lead for the leveloff depends on the rate of climb. Generally, a 10% lead is sufficient. For example, if the rate of climb is 500 f.p.m., you should begin to level off approximately 50 feet (10% of 500) below the desired altitude. Maintain climb power until you accelerate to cruise speed, then reduce power to the cruise setting. Finally, trim control pressures to hold the aircraft in a level flight attitude.

Lead your leveloff by 10% of the established rate of climb.

DESCENTS

You will practice descents to learn the techniques used for losing altitude without gaining excessive airspeed, controlling the rate of descent

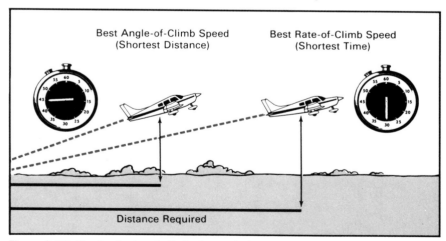

Figure 2-12. The best rate-of-climb airspeed allows you to gain altitude faster than any other speed. The best angle-of-climb speed results in the greatest altitude gain in the shortest distance.

with power and attitude, and converting altitude into as much distance as possible without the use of power. Initially, you will practice descents at the airspeed used for approaches to landings. After you learn this type of descent, you will practice the cruise descent. Since a cruise descent is flown at cruise airspeed, you will maintain a higher groundspeed.

ESTABLISHING THE DESCENT AT APPROACH SPEEDS

Descents usually require an adjustment to both pitch and power.

Usually you apply carburetor heat as the first step in establishing a descent. Many airplane manufacturers recommend using carburetor heat when you fly for long periods at low power settings. Next, reduce power to a predetermined setting or to idle. As you reduce power, apply back pressure gradually to the control wheel until the airplane slows to the desired descent speed. When you reach the descent airspeed, lower the nose attitude to the descent attitude that holds this airspeed. After you have established the proper descent attitude, trim the airplane. In many airplanes, the descent attitude is nearly the same as that used for straight-and-level cruising flight. [Figure 2-13]

Because the airflow over the controls is less rapid than at cruise airspeed and there is little propeller slipstream over the empennage, the controls tend to feel soft or mushy and less positive in response. You can learn to use this "feel" to help determine when the airplane is flying slowly. The feel you will develop in practicing descents is important to approach and landing practice.

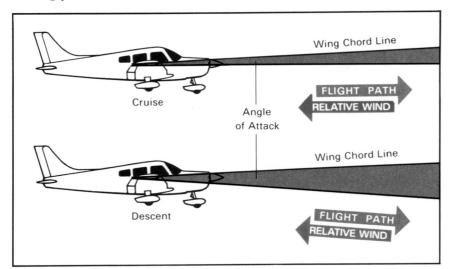

Figure 2-13. To produce lift at slower airspeeds, the wing must be at a higher angle of attack. To attain the higher angle of attack during a descent, maintain a near-level attitude.

MAINTAINING THE DESCENT

Use the airspeed indicator, altimeter, heading indicator, turn coordinator, and vertical speed indicator during the descent, as in other maneuvers. After you have established the desired descent attitude and trimmed the airplane properly, you should refer to these instruments to confirm that the airspeed, heading, and rate of descent are correct. If adjustment is required, make an attitude adjustment (either visual or instrument), permit the attitude to stabilize, and then refer to the appropriate instruments to confirm that you are descending as desired.

CONTROLLING THE RATE OF DESCENT

If you wish to maintain a constant airspeed descent, control the rate of descent with power. You will need to hold the pitch attitude slightly higher as you add power. On the other hand, if you have reduced power, you must lower the pitch attitude slightly to maintain a given airspeed. When power is added, propeller slipstream over the elevator (or stabilator) increases; therefore, a small trim adjustment is necessary. You can monitor the rate of descent by referring to the vertical speed indicator when your descent is well established and the instrument has settled to an accurate indication.

In a constant airspeed descent, use power to control the rate of descent.

USE OF FLAPS

You can increase the angle of descent by using flaps. You may also need to make moderate trim adjustments. Make descents with flaps retracted when you need maximum range or distance. When you wish rapid dissipation of altitude, use a full-flap, power-off glide. [Figure 2-14]

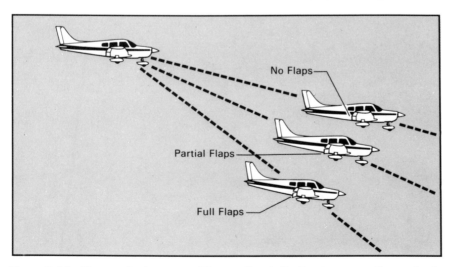

Figure 2-14. At a constant power setting, as flap deflection increases, the angle of descent also increases.

LEVELOFF FROM THE DESCENT

Lead your descent level-off by 10% of the rate of descent.

To return to straight-and-level flight, begin the transition before you reach the desired altitude. As with a climb, begin the leveloff at an altitude equal to 10% of the rate of descent by adjusting the nose position to level flight and simultaneously adding power to the cruise setting. Refer to wing and nose positions in order to maintain the proper attitude throughout the transition from descent to straight-and-level flight. Since adding power and increasing airspeed produce a moderate tendency to pitch upward, adjust the trim to relieve forward control pressures as you attain straight-and-level flight.

CHECKLIST ━━━━━━━━━━━━━━━━━━━━━━━━━━

After studying this section, you should have a basic understanding of:

✓ **Climbs** — How to establish, maintain, and level off from a climb.

✓ **Climb speed** — The meaning of best rate-of-climb, best angle-of-climb, and cruise climb speeds.

✓ **Descents** — How to establish, maintain, and level off from a descent.

✓ **Constant airspeed descents** — How to control the rate of descent when airspeed must be held constant.

✓ **Flaps** — Why flaps are beneficial during a descent.

TURNS

Turns generally are described by the number of degrees of bank necessary to produce them. A medium bank turn is one in which the airplane tends to hold a constant bank angle without control force on the ailerons. For training airplanes, 20° to 40° is a typical medium bank range, with 30° being most common.

ENTERING THE TURN

To roll into a bank, you apply aileron control pressure in the direction of the desired turn. For example, to execute a left turn, you turn the control wheel left to place the left aileron up and the right aileron down. How fast the airplane rolls depends on how much aileron control pressure you apply. How far the airplane rolls (the steepness of the bank) depends on how long you deflect the ailerons, since the airplane continues to roll as long as the ailerons are deflected. When the airplane reaches the desired angle of bank, neutralize the ailerons. [Figure 2-15]

The ailerons control the roll rate, as well as the angle of bank.

ELEVATOR CONTROL PRESSURES

When performing a turn, you must increase the pitch attitude slightly to increase the total lift. Therefore, the nose position you use to maintain the desired altitude is slightly higher in a turn than in level flight. The

During a turn, increased elevator back pressure is required to increase total lift.

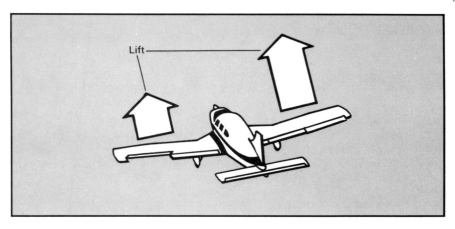

Lift

Figure 2-15. Turning the control wheel to the left causes the right wing to produce more lift and the left wing less. This causes the airplane to roll to the left.

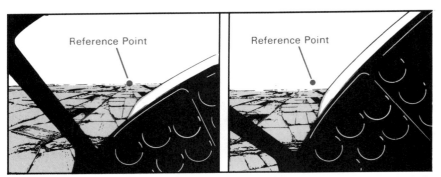

Figure 2-16. The proper reference for a medium bank turn is shown on the left. Notice how much higher the nose is for the steep bank turn shown on the right.

pitch attitude adjustment required for a medium bank turn is slight. However, steeper banks require a higher pitch attitude. [Figure 2-16]

COORDINATION OF CONTROLS

Apply sufficient rudder pressure to keep the ball of the inclinometer centered.

When you roll into a turn, the aileron on the inside of the turn is raised, and the aileron on the outside of the turn is lowered. As discussed in the *Private Pilot Manual*, the lowered aileron on the outside increases the angle of attack and produces more lift for that wing. Since induced drag is a by-product of lift, the outside wing also produces more drag than the inside wing. This causes a yawing tendency toward the outside of the turn, called adverse yaw. You use rudder pressure to counteract this tendency. [Figure 2-17]

You will hear the term "coordination" used when discussing turning techniques. This means you apply rudder pressure and aileron pressure simultaneously to properly counteract adverse yaw. The ball of the turn coordinator assists you in determining how much pressure is necessary. For a coordinated turn, the ball should remain in the center of the inclinometer. If the ball is not in the center, you should apply enough rudder pressure to center it. [Figure 2-18]

While the turn is in progress, you should occasionally check the altimeter, vertical speed indicator, and airspeed indicator to determine if corrections are necessary. If corrections are required, you should make necessary adjustments in steps. For example, if the nose is low, the airspeed high, and the altitude decreasing, increase pitch attitude to stop the descent and airspeed increase. When the airspeed has stopped increasing and the altitude has stabilized, make a slight nose-up pitch attitude adjustment to return to the desired altitude.

VISUAL REFERENCES IN THE TURN

When you make turns by visual reference, first apply coordinated aileron and rudder pressures in the direction you wish to turn. Notice that the

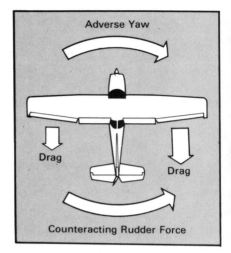

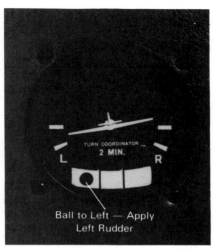

Figure 2-17. When the airplane is rolling to the left, adverse yaw attempts to move the nose to the right. Apply sufficient left rudder pressure to counteract this force.

Figure 2-18. In this example, the ball is located left of center. Therefore, apply sufficient left rudder pressure to center the ball.

nose of the airplane appears to move in an arc with respect to the horizon. You can determine when you have reached the proper bank angle by observing the angle of the cowling and instrument panel with respect to the horizon. [Figure 2-19]

ROLLING OUT OF THE TURN

Lead your roll-out by an amount equal to one-half your bank angle. For example, in a 20° bank turn, begin your roll-out approximately 10° before you reach the desired heading by applying coordinated aileron and rudder pressure. At the same time, begin releasing the back pressure on the control wheel so aileron, rudder, and elevator pressures are neutralized when the airplane reaches the wings-level position.

Figure 2-19. Both of these banks are approximately 15°. The nose position appears different during left and right turns because you sit to the left side of the centerline of the airplane.

TURNS BY INSTRUMENT REFERENCE

For turns by instrument reference, simply substitute the attitude indicator for the natural horizon.

After practicing turns by visual reference, you will learn to perform turns using instrument reference. Control pressures are applied in the same manner as when you use visual references, and the indications of the instruments are interpreted in the same way.

PERFORMING THE TURN

To establish a 15° turn, bank the airplane and apply coordinated rudder pressure until the 15° position is aligned with the bank index at the top of the attitude indicator. Then, neutralize aileron and rudder pressures and adjust the pitch attitude slightly upward, using additional back pressure on the control wheel. [Figure 2-20]

Make corrections in the same manner as when you are using visual references. However, adjust the attitude by using the attitude indicator and scan the other instruments to verify that the turn is progressing as you desire. One advantage of performing turns by instrument reference is that the nose position on the attitude indicator looks the same during left and right turns. Recover from the turn by applying coordinated aileron and rudder pressure, releasing the back pressure, and reestablishing straight-and-level flight by reference to the attitude indicator.

Figure 2-20. This is how your instruments appear once you are established in a level 15° banked turn to the left. Notice how the nose of the miniature airplane is elevated slightly above the horizon line.

STANDARD-RATE TURNS

The angle of bank frequently used in making turns by instrument reference is one that results in a standard-rate turn. A **standard-rate turn** produces a turn rate of three degrees per second. These turns are made by referring to the turn coordinator. [Figure 2-21]

A standard-rate turn is a turn of 3° per second.

ANGLE OF BANK REQUIRED FOR STANDARD-RATE TURN

The angle of bank necessary to produce the standard-rate turn is strictly a function of the true airspeed — the greater the airspeed, the greater the angle of bank needed to maintain a standard-rate turn. Training airplanes typically maintain cruise true airspeeds of approximately 100 to 110 knots. The angle of bank required for a standard-rate turn is approximately 15° to 17° at these speeds. The following list shows some typical speeds and the required bank angles for standard-rate turns:

True Airspeed	Approximate Bank Angle
100 knots	15°
110 knots	17°
120 knots	18°
130 knots	20°

TIMED TURNS

By using a standard rate, you can determine the amount of time required to make a turn before you initiate it. First, determine the number of

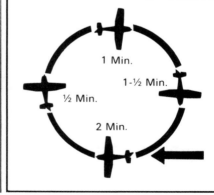

Figure 2-21. When the wing of the miniature airplane is aligned with the index, you will be turning at a rate of 3° per second and will complete a standard-rate turn of 360° in two minutes. If the wing of the miniature airplane is midway between the level flight position and the standard-rate position, you are performing a one-half standard-rate turn, or a turn of 360° in four minutes.

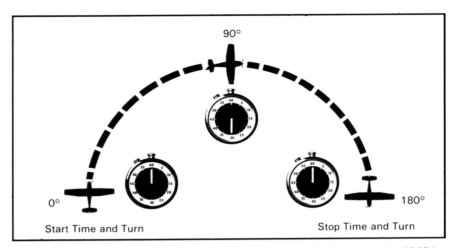

Figure 2-22. To determine the time it will take to make a 180° turn, divide 180° by 3. It takes 60 seconds to perform this turn.

degrees to be turned and divide by three. Then, note the time according to the second hand on the airplane clock and roll into the turn using the proper angle of bank for a standard-rate turn. Roll out to level flight when the predetermined amount of time has elapsed. [Figure 2-22]

COMBINATIONS OF FUNDAMENTAL MANEUVERS

As discussed earlier, straight-and-level flight, climbs, descents, and turns are the four fundamental flight maneuvers upon which you base all others. If you develop a thorough understanding of these basic elements and maintain effective and precise control of the airplane when you are performing each maneuver, you will develop a high level of proficiency as you continue your flight training.

As soon as you are proficient in climbs, descents, and turns, you will be introduced to climbing and descending turns to predetermined headings and altitudes. You will practice these combination maneuvers using both visual and instrument references.

CLIMBING TURNS

The objective of practicing climbing turns is to smoothly combine the techniques of climbs with those of turns. To perform a climbing turn, establish the climb as previously discussed. When climb power and attitude are set, roll to the desired bank angle. This is a two-step procedure initially; however, as you gain experience and proficiency, you will enter the maneuver by simultaneously establishing the climb attitude and the proper bank.

You should use the same airspeed for straight climbs and climbing turns. However, your rate of climb will be less for climbing turns than straight climbs. Generally, you perform climbing turns using shallow bank angles, because steep bank angles divert more of the vertical component of lift, which causes a reduction in rate of climb.

During maneuvers, you will find that you rarely reach the desired heading and altitude at the same time. If you reach the desired heading first, level the wings and maintain the climb until you reach the desired altitude. On the other hand, if you reach the altitude first, lower the nose to a level flight attitude and continue the turn to the desired heading. If you reach both the desired heading and altitude at the same time, you can perform these procedures simultaneously.

DESCENDING TURNS

Descending turns to preselected headings and altitudes combine the procedures for straight descents with those used in turns. Enter the decent using either visual or instrument references in the manner previously outlined for the straight descent. When you have established the descent attitude, roll to the desired angle of bank. As with climbing turns, initially perform the procedure in two steps. As you gain proficiency, you will learn to establish the descent attitude and bank simultaneously. As in any maneuver, you should trim off control pressures as required to maintain the selected attitude.

Use power to control the rate of descent. Make the initial power setting for the desired rate of descent and allow the pitch attitude and the rate of descent to stabilize. If you desire a higher rate of descent, reduce power. In contrast, you must add power if you desire a lower rate of descent.

Maintain the same airspeed in descending turns as in straight descents. However, your rate of descent will be higher in a descending turn than in a straight descent with a comparable power setting, because the vertical lift component is less when the airplane banks. You can compensate for this with a slight addition of power.

CHECKLIST ━━━━━━━━━━━━━━━━━

After studying this section, you should have a basic understanding of:

✓ **Turn entry and roll-out** — How to use the ailerons, elevator, and rudder in a coordinated manner when entering and exiting turns.

✓ **Standard-rate turn** — What it is and how to determine when the airplane is making a standard-rate turn.

✓ **Climbing and descending turns** — How to combine turns, climbs, and descents smoothly to enter and level off from climbing and descending turns.

SECTION D

TRAFFIC PATTERNS

The purpose of the standardized traffic pattern is to improve both the safety and efficiency of operations conducted at airports not served by a control tower. Normally, turns in a traffic pattern are made to the left. This pattern is called a **left-hand pattern**. You will find variations from the described pattern at different localities and at airports with control towers. For example, a **right-hand pattern** may be designated to expedite the flow of traffic when obstacles or concentrations of population make the use of a left-hand pattern undesirable.

TRAFFIC PATTERN LEGS

A normal traffic pattern is rectangular and has five named legs; downwind, base, final, upwind, and crosswind. Each traffic pattern also has a designated altitude at which the pattern is to be flown. [Figure 2-23]

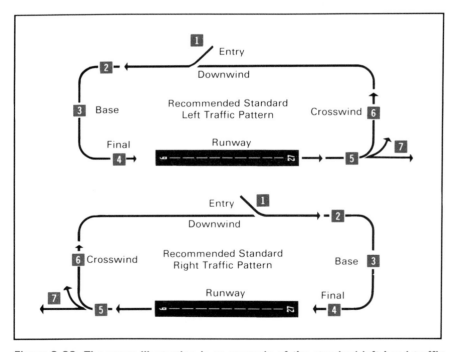

Figure 2-23. The upper illustration is an example of the standard left-hand traffic pattern. The lower one depicts a right-hand pattern. The numbered callouts in this illustration are fully explained in the following text.

PATTERN ENTRY

Traffic pattern entry procedures at an airport with an operating control tower are specified by the tower operator. At uncontrolled airports, traffic pattern altitudes and entry procedures may vary according to established local procedures. Usually, you enter the pattern at a 45° angle to the downwind leg, abeam the midpoint of the runway, and at a pattern altitude which is normally 1,000 feet above the ground (item 1). It is important to use the appropriate advisory frequency to obtain local weather, traffic, and landing information prior to entering the pattern. (Communications are covered later in this section.) At an uncontrolled airport, you may be the one to determine which runway to use, depending on the type of services available. In many cases, your decision will be based on the wind direction indicator.

DOWNWIND LEG

Fly the downwind leg (item 2) parallel to the runway and at the designated traffic pattern altitude. For most training airplanes, the appropriate distance from the runway is about one-half to one mile. If it becomes necessary to maneuver to maintain spacing with another airplane, only shallow "S" turns should be used, since traffic following you cannot anticipate major maneuvers such as a 360° turn. Normally, you begin the descent for landing when the airplane is abeam the touchdown point. However, you may need to delay the start of the descent if the downwind leg must be extended to follow traffic.

BASE LEG

Normally, you turn onto the base leg when the touchdown point is approximately 45° behind the inside wing tip. However, the base leg (item 3) must be adjusted according to other traffic and wind conditions. For example, if the wind is very strong, begin the turn sooner than normal. One important objective of the base leg is to allow the airplane to roll out on final approach at a distance no closer than one-quarter mile from the end of the runway, at an altitude appropriate to the glide path being flown.

The base leg should allow you to turn final no closer than one-quarter mile from the end of the runway.

FINAL APPROACH

The final approach (item 4) is the path the airplane flies immediately prior to touchdown. Since it is flown along an imaginary extension of the centerline of the runway, you must compensate for any crosswind conditions. If the approach does not terminate in a full-stop landing, climb out straight ahead, then follow the procedures outlined for the takeoff leg.

TAKEOFF LEG

The takeoff leg (item 5) normally consists of the airplane's flight path after takeoff. This leg is also called the upwind leg. Fly the airplane directly above an imaginary extension of the runway centerline and do not permit it to drift to one side or the other. Normally, you continue along this leg, without turning, until you reach an altitude within 300 feet of pattern altitude. Under certain conditions, such as high density altitudes or the existence of special airport procedures, you may need to start a turn at a somewhat lower altitude. Never start a turn at an altitude which, in your opinion as the pilot in command, is unsafe.

CROSSWIND LEG

Begin the crosswind leg (item 6) after you pass the departure end of the runway and have achieved a safe altitude. Also, be sure to check for other traffic in the pattern before starting your turn to crosswind, since you may have to extend your upwind leg to follow another aircraft. Ideally, as you turn from crosswind to downwind, the airplane is once again at the appropriate traffic pattern altitude.

A common misconception is that an airplane may stall when it turns downwind, since the wind shifts from a headwind to a tailwind. Although the groundspeed of the airplane is increased when turning downwind, the airspeed does not change. A stall that occurs during a turn to downwind, or to any other leg, is usually due to a pilot becoming distracted and failing to properly monitor the instruments and fly the airplane.

TRAFFIC PATTERN DEPARTURE

Always comply with the published departure procedures for any uncontrolled airport.

When a control tower is in operation, you can request and usually will receive approval for just about any type of departure. For example, you might request a straight-out, downwind, or right-hand departure. As a courtesy to the tower operator, make your departure request when you ask for takeoff clearance. At airports without an operating control tower, you must comply with the departure procedures established for that airport. These procedures usually are posted by airport operators so you can become familiar with the local rules. The standard procedure is either to fly straight-out or to make a 45° turn in the direction of the pattern after you reach a safe altitude (item 7).

COMMUNICATIONS

At airports with operating control towers, you are required by regulations to establish contact with the tower and obtain a clearance prior to entering the airport traffic area. Likewise, a clearance must be obtained prior to taxiing onto the runway for takeoff.

When you are within 10 miles of an uncontrolled airport, monitor the published CTAF, if your aircraft is radio equipped.

At airports without control towers, you are not required to have or use a radio. However, if you are radio equipped, using your radio greatly enhances safety. When inbound and about 10 miles out, obtain the local weather, runway conditions, and traffic information from the FSS located at the field or from the UNICOM operator, as appropriate. Then, switch to the published common traffic advisory frequency (CTAF) for that airport. This frequency is usually, but not always, the same frequency used to obtain airport information.

Monitor CTAF for a short period of time before you transmit to get a picture of the traffic situation and determine the best procedure for entering the pattern. Then, report your aircraft identification, position, and intentions. Always remember to include the name of the airport in your broadcasts, since more than one airport may be assigned the same CTAF.

When you depart, obtain airport information first, then monitor CTAF. Finally, when the runway and approach path are clear, announce your intentions and take off. On departure, monitor CTAF until you are about 10 miles from the airport.

TRAFFIC PATTERN COURTESIES

Occasionally, a number of airplanes may be in the traffic pattern practicing takeoffs and landings at the same time. If they all assume normal spacing, they may completely block other airplanes attempting to enter the pattern or take off from the airport. If you see this happening, you should extend your traffic pattern to accomodate the other airplane.

COLLISION AVOIDANCE

The primary responsibility for collision avoidance rests with you, the pilot in command. Although several systems have been designed as safety aids, nothing can replace vigilance. Airport operations require a constant effort to see and avoid other aircraft. You should make a point of checking both the approach and departure paths prior to takeoff or landing.

Here are some other procedures you can use at both controlled and uncontrolled airports to enhance your visibility. Use anticollision and landing lights in the pattern and within a 5- to 10-mile radius of the airport. During climbout, accelerate the airplane to cruise climb speed as soon as you reach a safe altitude. The higher speed results in a lower pitch attitude and increased forward visibility. In addition, avoid turns of more than 90° while you are in the traffic pattern. Also, prior to commencing any turn, check for traffic.

CHECKLIST ━━━━━━━━━━━━━━━━━━━

After studying this section, you should have a basic understanding of:

✓ **Traffic pattern legs** — What they are and how they are flown.

✓ **Traffic pattern entry** — What the proper procedures for entering the traffic pattern are.

✓ **Traffic pattern departure** — What the procedures for departing the traffic pattern are.

✓ **Communications** — Who you should contact and when you should establish contact.

CHAPTER 3

TAKEOFFS AND LANDINGS

INTRODUCTION

Few aspects of your training will be as satisfying and rewarding as mastery of takeoffs and landings. While learning these maneuvers, you must apply all of the basic skills you acquired in the early phases of your training program. Each takeoff and landing is a new challenge. In addition to varying wind conditions, the runway surface, length, and obstructions differ at every airport. When you master the basic traffic pattern skills, you are well prepared for takeoffs and landings under this wide variety of conditions.

NORMAL AND CROSSWIND TAKEOFFS

The checklists and takeoff procedures outlined in this section are provided as general guidelines only. Be sure to consult the pilot's operating handbook for your airplane for the proper checklists and procedures.

PRETAKEOFF CHECK

Use a written checklist whenever possible.

Before each takeoff, it is important for you to perform a pretakeoff check of the airplane equipment and systems to ensure proper operation. Use a written checklist provided by the airplane manufacturer or operator. This ensures that each item is checked in the proper sequence and that nothing is omitted.

After you taxi the airplane to the runup area, position it so the propeller blast is not directed toward other aircraft. If possible, point the nose into the wind to improve engine cooling. To prevent damage to the propeller and other parts of the airplane, avoid engine runups on loose gravel and sand.

During the pretakeoff check, which is sometimes referred to as the runup, divide your attention between the cockpit and the area around the airplane. If the parking brake slips, or you do not hold the toe brakes firmly, the airplane can move forward while your attention is inside the cockpit.

If you notice an abnormal condition prior to flight, delay the flight until the problem is resolved.

Usually, the engine will have warmed sufficiently before the pretakeoff check so it will accelerate smoothly when you apply power. All engine instrument indications must be normal before takeoff. If you observe any abnormal condition during the runup, return the airplane for maintenance, since even minor malfunctions can affect the safety and efficiency of the flight. Let's follow through a typical pretakeoff checklist.

1. Check that the cabin doors are securely closed and latched.
2. Check the flight controls to determine that they move correctly, freely, and easily throughout their total travel. A small movement of the controls is not sufficient; move each control through its full range of travel while noting the direction of movement.
3. Set the elevator trim to the TAKEOFF position.
4. Set the throttle to the r.p.m. recommended by the manufacturer for the power check.
   a. Move the carburetor heat to the ON position and note the power loss, then return it to the OFF position. With hot air entering the carburetor, the engine r.p.m. should decrease, indicating the carburetor heat is functioning.

b. Test the magnetos by noting the r.p.m with the magneto switch in the BOTH position, then move the magneto switch to the RIGHT position and note the r.p.m drop. Next, return the magneto switch to BOTH, then switch to the LEFT position and again note the r.p.m drop. Finally, return the magneto switch to the BOTH position for takeoff. The airplane manufacturer specifies the maximum permissible r.p.m. reductions for each magneto, as well as the maximum differential. For example, a manufacturer may specify that each magneto may not drop more than 150 r.p.m., and that the maximum difference between the two may not exceed 75 r.p.m.

c. Check the engine instruments. With the exception of the oil temperature gauge, they should register operation in the green arcs. Oil temperature may not indicate in the normal range until after takeoff. However, the airplane is considered ready for takeoff if the engine accelerates normally, the oil pressure remains steady and normal, and other engine instruments continue to register normally.

d. Check the suction gauge for a normal indication. A low reading may indicate a dirty air filter. Unreliable gyro indications may result if sufficient suction is not maintained.

5. Check and set the flight instruments, systems, and radios.

a. Set the altimeter to the altimeter setting supplied by the tower controller, or to the correct field elevation if you are operating from an uncontrolled field.

b. Set the heading indicator to coincide with the magnetic compass.

c. Check all gyro instruments for stable operation.

d. Check the ammeter or loadmeter for proper indication.

e. Set the radios to the desired frequencies.

f. Set the course selectors to the desired courses or radials.

When the checklist is complete, you are ready for takeoff. Before you taxi onto the runway, be sure to check both the approach and departure paths for traffic. At an uncontrolled field, be sure to check the entire area for other traffic as well. When the runway is clear, taxi the airplane into the takeoff position. At controlled airports, you must obtain a takeoff clearance from the control tower prior to taxiing onto the runway.

TAXIING INTO TAKEOFF POSITION

When you are ready for takeoff, taxi onto the runway, line up with the runway centerline, center the nosewheel, and neutralize the ailerons. After checking the windsock to determine the wind position in relation to the runway, you are ready to begin the takeoff roll.

Place your right hand on the throttle and keep it there throughout the takeoff. This assures that the throttle does not vibrate back during the takeoff roll. It also allows you to close the throttle quickly if you decide to abort the takeoff. Your feet should be resting on the floor with the

Proper placement of your hands and feet during the takeoff roll improves airplane control and safety.

balls of your feet on the bottom edges of the rudder pedals. This places your feet in a position where they have no tendency to press the toe brakes inadvertently.

TAKEOFF PROCEDURES

Begin the takeoff roll with a smooth application of power. As soon as you apply power and the airplane begins to roll, select a point on the cowl through which the runway centerline passes and use it as a reference for directional control. In addition, check the engine instruments to ensure the engine is developing full power and operating within limits. Slow acceleration or any hesitation in power is sufficient reason to discontinue the takeoff.

During the takeoff roll, maintain directional control with the rudder pedals; use the neutral aileron position if the wind is straight down the runway. The rudder pedals control the steerable nosewheel and are usually sufficient to maintain directional control; however, the rudder itself becomes more effective as you increase speed. Because of this, the amount of rudder deflection required for directional control changes throughout the takeoff roll. Before you add power, the rudder is neutral. As you add power, apply right rudder pressure to counteract engine torque. As speed increases and the controls become more effective, reduce rudder pressure to maintain directional control and apply slight back pressure to the control wheel. Establish the takeoff attitude at the speed specified in the pilot's operating handbook. In most training airplanes, this attitude is similar to the normal climb attitude.

The takeoff attitude is important because it is a compromise between holding the nose on the ground and selecting an attitude which is too nose-high. If the nosewheel is held on the ground too long, the airplane tends to build excess airspeed, which increases the length of runway required for takeoff. With an excessively nose-high attitude, the airplane may be forced into the air prematurely and then settle back to the runway. Also, it may be at such a high angle of attack (high drag condition) that it cannot accelerate to the liftoff airspeed. With the proper attitude, the airplane attains a safe speed and becomes airborne near the proper climb speed. If you hold that attitude after liftoff, the airplane accelerates to climb speed. Another advantage of maintaining this attitude is that the airplane will be in the best attitude to accelerate to climb speed if it is lifted into the air prematurely by a wind gust.

The speed used for initial climb after takeoff varies with local conditions. The initial climb speed varies, based on flap position and obstacles in the departure path. You may need to fly at the obstacle clearance speed, best angle-of-climb speed, or best rate-of-climb speed. The correct speed for each airplane and operating condition is specified in the pilot's operating handbook. When the airplane reaches the correct climb speed, adjust the pitch attitude to maintain this speed. During the climb, fly the takeoff leg of the traffic pattern straight out on an extension of the runway centerline without drifting to one side or the other.

CROSSWIND TAKEOFF

During practice of takeoffs, one of the factors which you must consider is the effect of a crosswind. The term **crosswind component** refers to that part of the wind velocity that acts at a right angle to the airplane's path on takeoff or landing. Most airplanes have a maximum demonstrated crosswind component listed in the POH. Of course, your personal crosswind limit is based on your skill level as well as any limitation set forth by your instructor during training. A crosswind component chart is used to calculate the crosswind component under a given set of conditions. It also allows you to calculate the **headwind component**, which may be used to adjust takeoff and landing performance figures. [Figure 3-1]

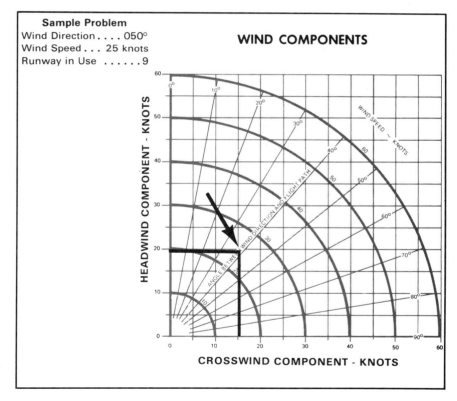

Figure 3-1. First, determine the angle between the wind and runway (090° - 050° = 40°). Enter the crosswind component chart at the point where the angle of 40° meets the wind speed of 25 knots. Proceed horizontally to the left and read the headwind component of 19 knots, or move vertically down and read the crosswind component of 16 knots.

Ailerons and rudder are used to counteract the effect of a crosswind during takeoff and landing.

During the takeoff and landing rolls, a crosswind tends to push and roll the airplane to the downwind side of the runway. To compensate for this effect, use the ailerons the same way you do for crosswind taxiing. For slow airspeeds at the beginning of the takeoff roll, you should use full aileron deflection. The wind flow over the wing with the raised aileron tends to hold that wing down, while airflow under the wing with the lowered aileron tends to push that wing up. These factors counteract the rolling tendency caused by the crosswind. As the airplane accelerates, the ailerons become more effective. Reduce the deflection gradually, so it is just sufficient to counteract the rolling tendency.

The wind also attempts to weathervane the airplane. You can counteract this effect by rudder application. The weathervaning tendency is a result of the wind striking the vertical stabilizer and rudder surfaces which are a considerable distance from the center of gravity. This causes the nose of the airplane to turn into the wind. The amount of crosswind correction necessary depends on the crosswind component. With moderate crosswind components, the airplane is sensitive to side loads as it approaches liftoff speed. If your corrections are improper, they will place side loads on the landing gear.

It takes practice to determine how much aileron and rudder deflection is required to compensate for a crosswind. When you use the right amount, you feel no side load and the airplane tracks straight down the runway. Hold the airplane on the runway until you attain a slightly higher-than-normal liftoff speed. At this point, lift the airplane off the runway promptly and establish a normal climb attitude. This technique reduces the chance of the airplane being lifted off the runway prematurely by a sudden gust of wind before it has attained sufficient airspeed to remain airborne. [Figure 3-2]

TURBULENCE

Turbulence, caused by high winds or other atmospheric conditions in the vicinity of an airport, can decrease takeoff maneuverability and climb performance. Essentially, this is because it can increase the possibility of a stall. Therefore, increased climb speeds must be maintained after a takeoff in rough air.

SIMULATED TAKEOFF EMERGENCIES

Although an engine malfunction on takeoff is rare, the possibility does exist. Therefore, you will learn ways to handle this situation during flight training. The simulated emergency situation occurs when your instructor reduces engine power by smoothly closing the throttle. The objective of this practice is to prepare you to meet the problems of an engine failure on takeoff. It helps you develop judgment, technique, confidence, and the ability to respond quickly and accurately to situations requiring prompt action.

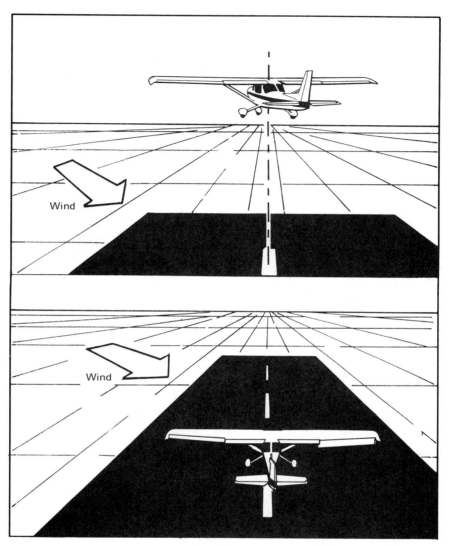

Figure 3-2. As speed increases during takeoff and ailerons become effective, reduce aileron pressure until there is just enough to counteract the crosswind. When the airplane is airborne and you have established a positive rate of climb, enter a crab by making a coordinated turn into the wind. This technique allows the airplane to track straight out on an imaginary extension of the runway centerline.

One emergency you might encounter is an engine malfunction on the takeoff roll or just after liftoff. If you suspect a malfunction during the takeoff roll, abort the takeoff quickly by moving the throttle to the idle position. Use the brakes as necessary to stop the airplane, and use the rudder to maintain directional control.

Should an engine fail at low altitude after takeoff, you must land straight ahead, making only small turns.

If your airplane has become airborne when the simulated emergency occurs, you should reduce the pitch attitude slightly and allow the airplane to settle back to the ground. Generally, if the airplane is low and power is lost, you have no choice but to continue straight ahead, making only small changes in direction to avoid obstacles. This technique is necessary because insufficient altitude is available to make a power-off 180° turn to return to the airport for a landing.

CHECKLIST

After studying this section, you should have a basic understanding of:

✓ **Pretakeoff check** — What the procedures are to ensure a properly operating airplane prior to flight.

✓ **Takeoff procedures** — What the procedures are to initiate takeoff and to control the airplane during the takeoff roll and initial climb-out.

✓ **Crosswind takeoffs** — What the effects of a crosswind are on takeoff and how to compensate for these effects.

NORMAL AND CROSSWIND LANDINGS

The approach and landing is the phase of flight most pilots look forward to, because it represents a high degree of accomplishment. Proper execution of landings is important because it gives an indication of your ability to perform basic maneuvers, plan ahead, and divide your attention among several tasks.

EFFECTS OF WIND

Initially, your instructor will probably have you practice landings on calm days. In a no-wind situation, you can simply fly perpendicular or parallel to the runway to maintain a uniform traffic pattern. As your skill level increases, you will begin to fly in windy conditions. In order to maintain the desired path around the traffic pattern, you will need to make adjustments for the wind. These adjustments will vary for each leg of the traffic pattern. [Figure 3-3]

The effects of wind on turns and on the final approach are covered, as appropriate, in the following discussion. Later, you will practice ground reference maneuvers, which will allow you to perfect your wind correction techniques.

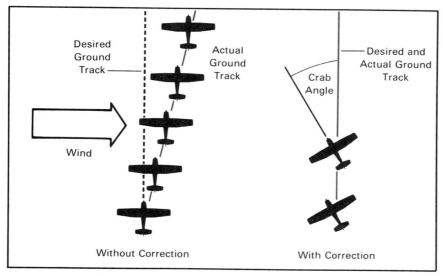

Desired Ground Track

Actual Ground Track

Wind

Without Correction

Crab Angle

Desired and Actual Ground Track

With Correction

Figure 3-3. To correct for the wind's effects, make a coordinated turn so the aircraft's nose is directed into the wind. The angle between the airplane's nose and the desired path over the ground is called the crab angle. As the wind tends to blow you away from your desired ground track, the crab angle allows you to maintain it.

APPROACH AND LANDING

A landing is nothing more than the transition of the airplane from being an airborne vehicle to being a ground vehicle. When you have mastered the procedures and techniques of landing, you will be able to land the airplane consistently and safely on the area you have selected. This requires a high degree of planning that begins on the downwind leg.

If you use a different traffic pattern size, airspeed, flap setting, or rate of turn to base and final on each approach, you have a new problem to solve. Your chances of touching down consistently at the appropriate spot on the runway are much lower. Fly the traffic pattern so the distance of the downwind leg from the runway does not vary. In addition, your altitude, point of power reduction, and approach airspeed should be the same for each approach. The turns to base and final should be consistent. Then, you can use flaps and power to make minor corrections for position and to compensate for wind.

Each traffic pattern and approach should be flown in a consistent manner.

Throughout training, you should practice consistency and precise control of the airplane to reduce the number of variables in the landing approach. The following paragraphs describe a typical approach and landing in a training airplane.

DOWNWIND LEG

Fly the downwind leg at a distance appropriate to your airplane and local traffic requirements. For most training airplanes, this distance is about one-half to one mile from the runway in use. The airplane's ground track should parallel the runway, with no tendency to angle toward or drift away from it. Angling or drifting causes the traffic pattern to have an abnormal shape, which greatly influences the length of the base leg. When you approach the 180° point, or the point opposite the intended landing area, your airspeed should be near cruise in most training airplanes. In addition, your altitude should be at the designated traffic pattern altitude. This is usually 1,000 feet, unless specified otherwise. [Figure 3-4]

Use the approach speed recommended in the POH or, if none is given, use 1.3 V_{S0}.

When the airplane reaches approach airspeed, you normally maintain that speed and initiate the descent. However, you may need to delay the start of the descent if the downwind leg must be extended to follow traffic. The transition from cruise speed on downwind to descent speed is a practical application of the transition from cruise to descent that you learned earlier. The POH normally specifies the recommended approach speed. When an approach speed is recommended, you should maintain the speed as precisely as possible. If an approach speed is not recommended, use a final approach speed that is 1.3 times the power-off stall speed in the landing configuration (V_{S0}).

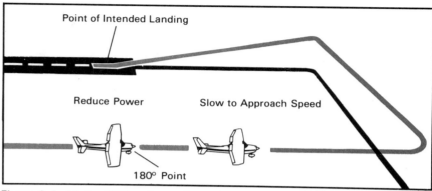

Figure 3-4. At the 180° point, reduce the power to the descent power setting, maintain altitude, and allow the airspeed to slow to approach speed.

BASE LEG

You usually begin the turn to base leg when the touchdown point is approximately 30° to 45° behind the wing. However, before beginning the turn, be sure to check for other traffic. [Figure 3-5]

With practice, this perspective becomes so familiar that you can detect the need for small corrections at this position. Vary the start of the turn to base leg to compensate for variations in conditions. Throughout the approach, you must be alert for other traffic in the pattern, especially on final approach. As you turn base, the wind tends to push the airplane farther away from the runway. Therefore, it is usually necessary to execute a turn of more than 90° to apply the necessary crab angle. Then, monitor your ground track, since further adjustments may be required.

When the airplane rolls out on base leg, it is at the point called the key position. When you reach this spot on each approach, you must assess your position and determine whether or not to make corrections in the approach pattern. [Figure 3-6]

Figure 3-5. From the downwind perspective, the runway will look similar to this view when it is time to begin your turn from downwind to base.

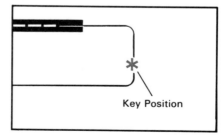

Figure 3-6. At the key position, evaluate your altitude, airspeed, distance from the runway, and wind. Then make any corrections needed to adjust the approach.

For example, if the airplane is high, it will land beyond the desired touchdown point. In this situation, there are two possible corrections— you can reduce power or extend additional flaps. You can use one or both, depending upon the amount of correction needed.

If the airplane is low or wide on base leg, or the wind is stronger than normal, you will also need to make corrections. Otherwise, the airplane will land short of the desired point. There are two actions that you can take to avoid this situation. You can begin the turn to final sooner than normal, or you can add power. You can use either one or both, depending on the amount of correction necessary. Retracting the flaps is not considered an acceptable correction. Normally, once you extend the flaps, they are not retracted until you have completed the landing or abandoned the landing approach.

Make corrections for position anytime you recognize a need. The significance of the key position is that it is an early decision point where you can easily make major adjustments. This ensures a smooth approach and avoids large or abrupt last-minute corrections. Throughout the approach, you should continue to assess your position relative to the runway to determine the need for additional corrections. Through the process of assessing your position, making corrections, and then reevaluating the touchdown point, you are able to judge your touchdown point accurately.

FINAL APPROACH

Complete the turn to final no closer than one-quarter mile from the runway.

Before you turn to the final approach leg, always look in all directions for other traffic. If the area is clear, make the turn to final. The turn to final is usually completed at a distance of at least one-quarter mile from the runway threshold. Normally, your altitude is about 300 to 400 feet AGL as you roll out on final. This may vary with the particular airplane or because of adjustments for other traffic in the pattern.

Based on existing wind conditions, you may have to begin the turn to final sooner or later than in a no-wind situation. Your objective is to complete the turn and roll out on the extension of the runway centerline. Maintain the approach airspeed as specified in the POH, or 1.3 V_{S0}, as appropriate. Monitor the approach speed until you begin the landing transition.

Do not adjust approach speed for nonstandard temperature or pressure.

The recommended approach speed is an indicated airspeed that should not be adjusted for various temperature and altitude combinations. Although temperature and pressure changes will change air density, and therefore lift, a given indicated airspeed will continue to ensure the same amount of lift.

Throughout the landing approach, your ability to use visual attitude references to control speed is the key to a good landing. You must be able to scan outside references while controlling the speed accurately. The pitch attitudes should look familiar, since they are the ones you used when you practiced straight descents and descending turns.

Your required rate of descent on final approach is directly affected by the headwind component. As the wind speed increases, your groundspeed decreases. This means you will need to decrease your rate of descent in order to reach the runway.

If you maintain a constant approach angle, the apparent shape of the runway will remain fixed. If your approach becomes shallower, the runway will appear to shorten and become wider. Conversely, if your approach is steepened, the runway will appear to be longer and narrower. Therefore, if you maintain a constant approach angle, the sides of the runway will maintain the same relationship and the threshold will remain in a fixed position in relation to the airplane's nose. [Figure 3-7]

During early landing practice, it is common to overcontrol the airplane. To avoid this, make smooth, positive corrections back to that pattern, whenever you notice a deviation. If you are low, for example, it is usually not necessary to make an abrupt correction and climb back to the standard pattern. Instead, you can add power and reduce the rate of descent and/or level off for a short period until you regain the correct approach angle.

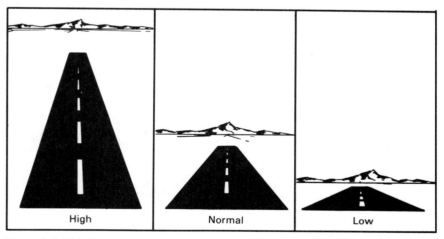

| High | Normal | Low |

Figure 3-7. This illustration shows how the apparent length and width of the runway vary with approach angle. By monitoring the shape of the runway, you can maintain a constant approach path.

Frequently, approach speed is near the best angle-of-glide speed. This means that any other airspeed results in a steeper angle of descent. If the airplane is short of the desired touchdown spot, you cannot stretch a glide by raising the nose and slowing the airspeed; instead, you must add power.

If the approach is extremely high, there is very little value in entering a steep descent. Although it appears the airplane will reach the chosen point of touchdown, the dive causes an increase in airspeed which must be dissipated in the flare. The result is that a greater distance is covered as the airplane floats down the runway, usually well beyond the selected touchdown point.

LANDING

The landing consists of three elements — the flare, the touchdown, and the roll-out. The term **flare** refers to the process of changing the attitude of the airplane from a glide or descent attitude to a landing attitude. Its purpose is to reduce speed and decrease the rate of descent.

The actual point at which the airplane will land is located some distance beyond the "aim" point used on final approach.

You can estimate the point at which the airplane will actually touch down. Find the point where the glide path intersects the ground and add the approximate distance to be traveled in the flare. The glide path intersection point, also called the aiming point, is the spot on the ground that has no apparent relative movement. As the airplane descends, all objects beyond the glide path intersection point appear to move away from the airplane, while objects closer appear to move toward it. The approximate distance traveled in the flare varies, depending on the approach speed and wind. [Figure 3-8]

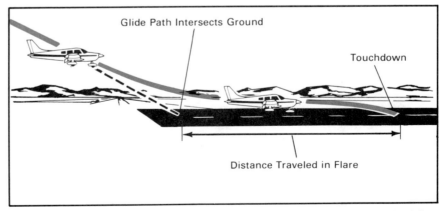

Figure 3-8. During the final approach, you will touch down several hundred feet beyond the aiming point. This allows the airplane to stabilize in the flare prior to touchdown.

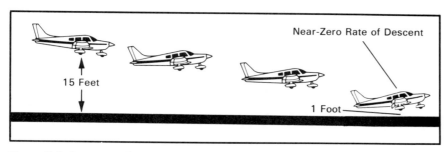

Figure 3-9. In preparation for landing, adjustments are made to the airplane's attitude, speed, and rate of descent during the flare.

The flare begins at different altitudes for airplanes of varying weights and approach speeds. However, for most training airplanes, it begins at approximately 10 to 20 feet above the ground. Initiate the flare with a gradual increase in back pressure on the control wheel to reduce speed and decrease the rate of descent. Ideally, the airplane reaches a rate of descent near zero, approximately one foot above the runway at about 8 to 10 knots above stall speed with idle power. [Figure 3-9]

Next, attempt to hold the airplane just off the runway by increasing back pressure. This causes the airplane to settle slowly to the runway in a slightly nose-high attitude as it approaches stall speed. The pitch attitude at touchdown should be very close to the pitch attitude at takeoff, with the nosewheel held clear of the runway. The main wheels should touch down beyond and within 500 feet of a point specified by your instructor. After touchdown, maintain back pressure and allow the nosewheel to touch down gently.

The cues you make use of in the flare and landing are a combination of visual and kinesthetic feelings. You have practiced descents and power-off stalls to build sensitivity to control responses and smoothness in preparation for the flare and landing. Generally, kinesthetic sensitivity is not developed fully at the time you begin landing practice; therefore, vision is the most important sense.

The altitude for the flare and the height throughout the flare are determined by your depth perception. **Depth perception** is the visual comparison of the size of known objects on the ground; therefore, the area where you focus your vision during the approach is important. If you focus too close to the airplane or look straight down, the airspeed blurs objects on the ground. This causes your actions to be delayed or too abrupt. When you focus too close to the airplane, the tendency is to overcontrol and level off too high.

If you focus too far down the runway, you will be unable to judge height above the ground accurately. Consequently, your reactions will be slow. In this situation, you will generally allow the airplane to fly onto the runway without flaring. Thus, it becomes obvious that you must focus at some intermediate point. A guideline is to focus about the same distance ahead of the airplane as when you are driving a car at the same speed. However, you must look to one side of the airplane, since its nose may block your view ahead during the flare and landing. [Figure 3-10]

During the roll-out, maintain directional control with rudder pressure. As the airplane touches down, your feet should be in the same position on the rudder pedals as they were during the flare. With your heels on the floor, there is no tendency to use the brakes inadvertently, but you will be able to reach them, if necessary.

GO-AROUND

A general rule of thumb in landing practice is that, if the airplane has not touched down in the first one-third of the runway, you should abandon the landing by flying around the traffic pattern and setting up another landing approach. This go-around procedure may also be required when an aircraft or some other obstacle is on the runway or when you feel the approach is uncomfortable, incorrect, or potentially dangerous.

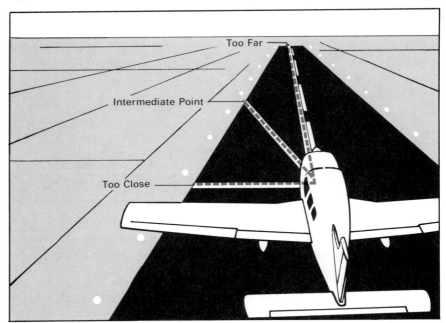

Figure 3-10. The flare and landing are made easier when you focus at the correct distance ahead of the airplane.

The decision to make a go-around should be positive; initiate the maneuver before a critical situation develops. Once you have made the decision, carry it out without hesitation. In many cases, the go-around is initiated with the airplane at a slow airspeed and in a nose-high attitude. In this situation, your first response is to apply all available power, then accelerate the airplane to the best angle-of-climb speed and adjust the pitch attitude. Once you reach a safe speed and altitude, retract the flaps. If another aircraft is on the runway during the go-around, make a gentle turn to the right side of the runway, if possible. [Figure 3-11]

Continue the climb on the takeoff leg parallel to the runway until you reach the crosswind leg. If another airplane is ahead, allow proper spacing and join the traffic pattern.

BOUNCED LANDING

At times, you may perform landings that cause the airplane to bounce into the air. Usually, it is wise not to attempt to salvage these landings. Instead, you should make an immediate go-around. Except when lowering flaps or trimming the airplane, you should have your hand on the throttle throughout the approach and landing. When a landing is bad, make a prompt decision to go around and add all available power. Adjust the pitch attitude to a normal climb attitude and complete the go-around procedures.

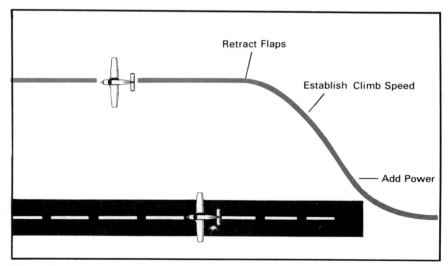

Figure 3-11. When you initiate a go-around with another airplane on the runway, adjust your flight path to be far enough to the side of the runway that it does not interfere with an airplane taking off. In this position, you can see the runway clearly. Special cases, such as use of parallel runways, may prevent you from making this slight turn or may require you to make a slight left turn.

When any doubt exists as to the successful outcome of an approach and landing, execute an immediate go-around.

If the airplane bounces only a small amount and gains just a few feet of altitude, hold the nose in the landing attitude while the airplane settles back to the runway. Use a similar procedure if the airplane "balloons" because the elevator has been pulled back too rapidly. After stopping the resulting climb, return the nose to the landing attitude and hold it in that attitude until the airplane settles on the runway. However, if you balloon too high or there is any question about the successful outcome of the landing, the best procedure is to go around.

USE OF WING FLAPS DURING LANDING

You can make landings with no flaps, partial flaps, or full flaps. The procedures used with various flap settings are generally the same; however, there are specific differences. With no flaps, the rate of descent usually is less than with partial flaps. To avoid this situation, you must adjust power and the traffic pattern. Since the stall speed with no flaps is higher than it is with full flaps, the airplane touches down at a faster speed and the landing roll-out is longer.

When you use full flaps for landing, you will typically extend the first increment of flaps on the downwind leg and the next on base leg. Usually, you will extend full flaps on the final approach leg. At the full-flap setting, the rate of descent increases, so the tendency is to land short. The touchdown speed is slower, since the full-flap stall speed is less than the no-flap or partial-flap stall speed. This results in a shorter ground roll.

If a go-around with full flaps is required, follow the procedures recommended in the pilot's operating handbook. After adding all available power, retract the flaps to an intermediate setting, if required, but do not attempt to enter a normal climb attitude immediately. Instead, use the straight-and-level, slow flight attitude which allows the airplane to maintain its present altitude. As you approach the best angle-of-climb speed, maintain that speed until all obstacles are cleared. Then, accelerate to the best rate-of-climb speed, slowly retract remaining flaps, and continue the departure just as you would a normal takeoff. During the initial stages of a go-around, be extra cautious. An attempt to raise the nose immediately may result in a stall. In addition, suddenly raising all of the flaps can cause the airplane to descend onto the ground.

CROSSWIND LANDING TECHNIQUE

The approach to landing in a crosswind is essentially the crosswind takeoff process in reverse. The turn to final should be completed on an extension of the runway centerline, with the airplane in a crab to correct for wind drift.

On final, lower the wing into the wind and use opposite rudder pressure to keep the nose pointed straight down the runway. This is referred to as a **side slip.** When you perform the slip properly, the airplane has no tendency to drift from one side of the runway to the other. Beginning pilots usually place the airplane in the wing-low condition at altitudes of 100 to 200 feet AGL while on final, but as they become more experienced, they tend to wait until just before they begin the flare. [Figure 3-12]

The airplane must contact the runway without drifting to either side. You must align both the ground track and the longitudinal axis of the airplane with the runway. If you do not, side loads will be imposed on the landing gear and tires, resulting in damage. As the airplane slows, the downwind wing will lower and the other wheel will touch the ground. As the airplane continues to slow, add more aileron, since the ailerons become less effective with speed loss.

In moderate and light crosswinds, the nose attitude for liftoff and touchdown is the same as in normal takeoffs and landings. In a strong crosswind, place the nose on the ground with positive elevator pressure to allow the nosewheel to assist in directional control. Take care not to lift the main landing gear off the runway as a result of excessive airspeed

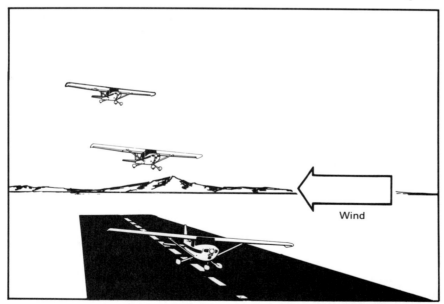

Wind

Figure 3-12. Start the flare at the normal altitude and hold the wing down throughout the flare and touchdown. This causes the airplane to touch down initially on one main wheel.

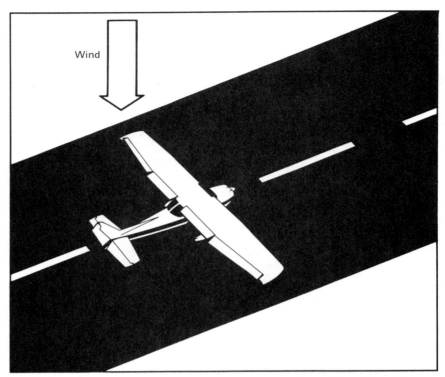

Wind

Figure 3-13. During the landing flare and roll-out, use the rudder to keep the nose of the airplane aligned with the centerline, and use the ailerons to control drift.

and control wheel pressure. In addition, aileron controls should be fully into the wind, not neutralized, at the end of the landing roll. [Figure 3-13]

In gusty wind conditions, you may use a slightly different landing technique. You can maintain better control if you fly the airplane onto the runway at an airspeed slightly higher than normal, then hold it on the runway with slight forward control wheel pressure. In a left-hand traffic pattern, when the wind is from the right side of the runway, the wind tends to distort the pattern by pushing the airplane wide on the downwind leg and slowing the groundspeed on the base leg. If you do not correct this condition, it will result in angling turns to final and approaches that are shallower or short of the runway.

When the wind is from the left of the landing runway, it tends to push the airplane closer to the runway and increase groundspeed on base leg. This situation may cause you to overshoot the final and results in approaches that are high and long. If you recognize these tendencies, you can take corrective action in the traffic pattern.

SLIPS

The slip is a flight attitude used to increase the angle of descent without causing an increase in airspeed. You accomplish this by exposing as much of the airplane surface to the oncoming air as possible, so the airplane's frontal area produces considerable drag. This allows a steeper angle of descent without acceleration. Flaps serve the same purpose, but they cannot always be used because of crosswinds or gusts. The two types are side slips and forward slips. They are aerodynamically the same, but they differ in the way you maneuver the airplane with respect to the ground.

SIDE SLIP

A side slip is used to compensate for drift during crosswind landings. To maintain a constant heading and a straight flight path, balance the aileron and rudder control pressure. Too much aileron or too little opposite rudder causes a turn in the direction of bank. In contrast, too much rudder or too little opposite aileron causes a yaw away from the bank. To steepen the descent, increase both aileron and rudder in a coordinated manner. [Figure 3-14]

FORWARD SLIP

The **forward slip** can be valuable when you are landing in fields with obstructions. In an airplane with side-by-side seating, you will usually slip to the left, since this provides you with an excellent view of the

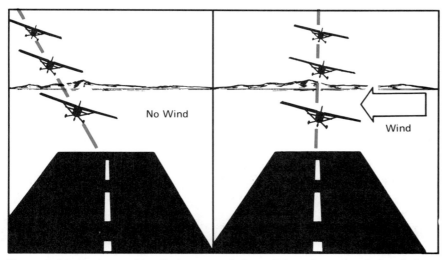

Figure 3-14. During a side slip in a no-wind condition, the nose of the airplane remains on the same heading throughout the maneuver, but the ground track is sideways in the direction of the low wing. However, when you perform a side slip into a crosswind, the resulting ground track is a straight line which is parallel to the longitudinal axis of the airplane.

Figure 3-15. To initiate a forward slip, lower one wing by using aileron control. At the same time, apply opposite rudder to keep the airplane from turning in the direction of the lowered wing. This procedure keeps the airplane's ground track in alignment with the extended centerline of the runway, but allows the nose of the airplane to angle away from the runway. To prevent the airspeed from increasing, raise the nose slightly above the normal gliding position. In this attitude, the glide path steepens, even though the airspeed remains constant.

landing area during the entire slip. However, if a crosswind is present, execute the slip into the wind. [Figure 3-15]

As soon as you lose sufficient altitude, begin the recovery. Raise the low wing and simultaneously ease rudder pressure as you level the wings and adjust pitch attitude to the normal glide attitude. The only difference between the control application in right and left slips is that the control pressures are reversed. You should perform forward slips with the engine at idle power, since using power decreases the rate of descent.

CHECKLIST

After studying this section, you should have a basic understanding of:

✓ **Key position** — What the importance of the key position is and how to adjust the approach from that point.

✓ **Landing** — How control of the airplane is maintained during the landing flare and roll-out, and the influence of ground effect.

✓ **Flaps** — How flaps are used in an approach and during a go-around.

✓ **Crosswind landings** — How to compensate for a crosswind in the traffic pattern and during final approach, landing, and roll-out.

EMERGENCY LANDING PROCEDURES

Since modern airplane engines are extremely reliable, actual mechanical malfunctions are rare. However, inadvertent fuel exhaustion or an actual engine component malfunction may require you to make an emergency landing. Five general steps used to cope with this type of situation are listed in sequence.

1. Establish the best glide speed.
2. Scan the immediate area for a suitable field.
3. Turn to a heading that will take the airplane to that field.
4. Attempt to determine the cause of the power failure and restart the engine, if possible. Follow an appropriate emergency checklist and declare an emergency.
5. Set up a landing approach to the selected field.

Emergency landing practice puts the airplane in a precarious position in the event of unforseen circumstances. For this reason, you should practice these procedures only when the instructor is in the airplane.

ESTABLISHING ATTITUDE AND GLIDE SPEED

If the engine fails, you should attempt to conserve altitude. Apply back pressure on the control wheel as you slow the airplane to the best glide speed. This speed is normally specified in the POH and is the speed which provides the greatest horizontal travel from a given altitude. As you reach the best glide speed, trim the airplane to relieve the control pressures and to aid in maintaining the proper attitude and airspeed. If the airspeed is below the best glide speed at the time of power failure, lower the nose immediately to obtain this speed and retrim the airplane. If the flaps are extended, increase the airspeed to a safe flap retraction speed, retract the flaps, establish the best glide speed, and retrim the airplane.

The first step after an engine failure is to establish the best glide speed.

SELECTING A FIELD

Select a field within the immediate area. As a general guideline, select a field that can be evaluated easily for obstructions and terrain, and one that is within gliding distance from your present altitude. If you select a field several miles from your present position, you may arrive to find it covered with rocks and trees and crisscrossed with several ditches or fences. You would have been better off to have selected a field within your immediate area.

There are many variables to consider in selecting a suitable field, including the wind direction and speed, length of the field, obstructions, and the surface condition. You must evaluate all these factors and decide which field provides the greatest possibility of a successful landing.

A long field positioned into the wind, with a firm, smooth surface that is free of obstructions, is the most desirable. However, all of these features are seldom available. On one occasion, it may be better to accept a crosswind landing on a long field, rather than attempt to land into the wind on a very short field. On another occasion, a downwind landing with light winds and no obstructions may be preferable to a landing into the wind with numerous obstructions.

MANEUVERING TO A FIELD

If you follow the previous suggestions, the field you select should be within easy gliding distance. This means the airplane should be headed directly toward the field, and any excess altitude should be dissipated near the field. From that vantage point, you are in a good position to observe the field carefully for wires, fences, holes, tree stumps, ditches, or other hazards that you did not observe clearly from a greater distance.

It is better to circle over a field than away from it.

It is inadvisable to circle away from the field, then try to make a long, straight-in glide to the field. The estimation of glide distance from a faraway point is difficult, even for experienced pilots. A circling approach over the field allows you to make adjustments for altitude and keeps you in a position from which you can reach the field.

DETERMINING CAUSE OF FAILURE

After you have set up the glide, selected the field, and headed the airplane for the field, you should attempt to find the cause of the malfunction and restart the engine, if possible. Loss of engine power that occurs suddenly is often caused by a fuel problem. Therefore, check to make sure the fuel selector is on and is set to a tank that has fuel.

Next, check the mixture to see that it is in the RICH position and, if the airplane is equipped with an auxiliary fuel pump, that it is turned ON. Apply carburetor heat early in the procedure to determine if ice has formed and to attempt to remove it. Then, check the magneto switch to see that it is in the BOTH position.

Always use an emergency checklist when one is provided.

After a quick check for obvious problems, you should carefully follow the appropriate emergency checklist. This serves two purposes. First, a checklist makes sure you have checked each item which may be responsible for the engine failure. Second, if you are still unable to restart the engine, a checklist will make sure you have the airplane properly configured for the emergency landing.

Be methodical, perform your checks in a definite sequence, and take time to be thorough. It may seem as though it takes minutes to accomplish this, but it requires only a few seconds to make an unhurried check. If you discover the cause of the power failure and remedy it, you will not need to use the starter to restart the engine, since the propeller continues to turn, or windmill, in a power-off glide.

Once you have prepared for the landing, use your radio to declare an emergency. Be sure to give your position as accurately as possible, as well as the type of airplane and number of persons on board.

EMERGENCY LANDING APPROACH

If you have planned correctly, the airplane should be at the 180° point when you reach a normal traffic pattern altitude. From that point, the approach is like a normal power-off approach. The value of this procedure is that it places you in a position where you have familiar points from which to judge glide angle, speed, and distances. [Figure 3-16]

Unfortunately, it is not always possible to reach the ideal position. You may have to use a right-hand pattern instead of a left-hand pattern because of your position. If the altitude at which power failure occurs is too low or the distance to a suitable landing field is too great, you may not be able to arrive at either a left or a right 180° position. If this situation occurs, the alternative is to plan the approach so the airplane can

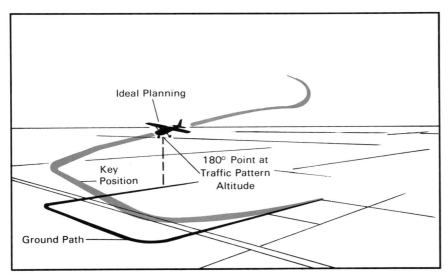

Figure 3-16. If you are able to maneuver the airplane to a normal downwind position, you should be able to use all of the normal cues to turn base leg, judge position, and turn to final.

intercept the normal traffic pattern. For example, the next best place for interception may be the key position. [Figure 3-17]

Use flaps as required during the approach. Full flaps should be used only after the turn to final is completed and you are assured of reaching the intended field.

During the landing, you must remember the distance traveled in the landing flare. For example, if the desired landing point is just beyond a ditch, the aiming point must be on the near side of the ditch. [Figure 3-18]

EMERGENCY LANDING PRACTICE

Since most practice emergency landing approaches terminate in a go-around, it is possible for you to fall into the habit of considering the procedure as just another training exercise. To avoid this, assume that each simulated emergency landing will actually result in a landing. Careful cultivation of this assumption will prepare you for the possibility that you may be required to perform an actual emergency landing.

If the selected field is an approved landing area, your instructor may require you to proceed and land. If the field is not approved, initiate a go-around when the instructor specifies. The altitude for the go-around

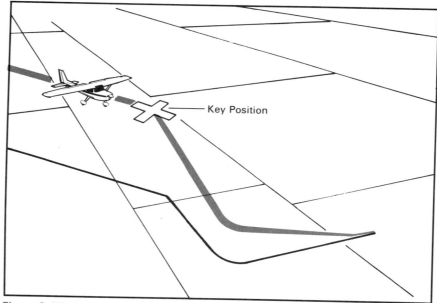

— Key Position

Figure 3-17. When the ideal pattern cannot be flown, you should try to visualize a normal traffic pattern overlying the chosen field. Then, consider the altitude and your position so you can plan to intercept the traffic pattern at the earliest point.

Figure 3-18. In this example, it appears that the airplane will touch down short of the intended point. During the flare, however, the airplane will glide across the ditch and land at the desired spot.

will be low enough so the outcome of the simulated emergency landing is apparent and high enough that safety is not compromised.

To initiate the go-around, apply all available power, place carburetor heat in the COLD position, and establish an airspeed at or above the best angle-of-climb. When you are well clear of all obstructions, retract the flaps and resume a normal climb. In order to conform with normal traffic pattern procedures, do not begin turns below 400 feet AGL.

PARTIAL POWER MALFUNCTIONS

In addition to practicing emergency landings, you must know how to cope with certain other situations. To practice these procedures, the instructor simulates or states a given problem, then demonstrates or explains the best corrective actions. These problems may include partial loss of power, rough engine operation, carburetor ice, fuel starvation, and fire in the engine compartment.

OTHER EMERGENCY PROCEDURES

In addition to partial or complete power malfunctions, you should become familiar with other system or equipment malfunctions. These should include inoperative electrical system, fire or smoke in the cabin, gear or flap malfunctions, door opening in flight, and inoperative elevator trim tab. You should be able to explain the causes, indications, and remedial actions for these and other malfunctions. You should also be familiar with the proper course of action in the event you become lost, are trapped on top of an overcast, lose radio communications, or encounter unanticipated adverse weather. Finally, whenever an emergency or abnormal situation develops, remain calm. Also, check to see if the manufacturer has a published checklist for the conditions. If one exists, it should be followed in a calm, methodical manner.

CHECKLIST

After studying this section, you should have a basic understanding of:

✓   **Engine failure or loss of power in flight** — What the possible causes of an engine failure are and the use of an appropriate emergency checklist.

✓   **Emergency landing field selection** — What factors to consider in selecting a suitable landing site.

✓   **Maneuvering to an emergency field** — What factors to consider to ensure a safe approach to and arrival at an emergency field.

✓   **Takeoff emergencies** — What procedures to follow in the event the engine fails during or shortly after takeoff.

✓   **Other emergencies** — How to determine the possible cause and remedial action for each condition.

ADVANCED MANEUVERS

INTRODUCTION

During flight training, you will learn maneuvers that cover the full scope of the airplane's handling characteristics and responses to control movements. Such maneuvers include flight at critically slow airspeeds, stalls, and constant altitude turns. The general purpose of these maneuvers is to teach you how the airplane responds and reacts in a variety of power, attitude, flap, and landing gear configurations. Practicing these maneuvers not only develops your perception, orientation, and proficiency, but also your feel for the airplane.

FLIGHT AT CRITICALLY SLOW AIRSPEEDS

Maneuvering at critically slow airspeeds (also referred to as slow flight or flight at minimum controllable airspeed) helps you develop a feel for the controls and an understanding of how load factor, pitch attitude, airspeed, and altitude control relate to each other. Knowledge of these relationships will aid you in maintaining proper airspeeds and pitch attitudes for changing flight conditions. It also helps you assess the reduction of control effectiveness during flight at slower-than-normal speeds and determine the power required for flight at different airspeeds.

During critically slow airspeed maneuvers, you should fly the airplane slightly above the stall speed. This speed must be sufficiently slow so any reduction in speed or power, or increase in load factor results in an immediate stall.

The procedures for entering the maneuver from cruise flight help develop smoothness and coordination of elevator (or stabilator), rudder, and power controls. The initial objective is to perform a smooth transition from cruise flight to critically slow airspeeds while maintaining altitude. Enter the maneuver at an altitude that will allow you to fly it no lower than 1,500 feet AGL.

Use a clearing turn to scan for traffic in your area.

Before you begin any maneuver which is not necessary for normal flight, you should execute a clearing turn. A **clearing turn** usually consists of at least a 180° change in direction. A typical method of executing this maneuver is to make two 90° turns in opposite directions. The clearing turn allows you to scan the local area for traffic which may be hidden by blind spots on your airplane.

ENTRY PROCEDURES

To enter the maneuver, first execute a clearing turn. Once the area is clear of traffic, apply carburetor heat if it is normally used when power is reduced, then reduce power several hundred r.p.m. (or several inches of manifold pressure) below the power setting required to maintain altitude. After reducing power, apply any necessary back pressure to the control wheel to maintain altitude as the airspeed decreases. If you apply back pressure too fast, the airplane climbs; if you apply it too slowly, the airplane descends. During this transition, use the trim to remove excess control wheel pressure.

When the airplane nears the desired pitch attitude and airspeed, increase power to a setting which will maintain altitude. Then make small power

Figure 4-1. These are the approximate visual and instrument pitch attitudes required during flight at critically slow airspeeds.

adjustments to maintain a constant altitude and retrim the airplane, as necessary, to remove control wheel pressures. [Figure 4-1]

As the airplane slows, you will also notice that the rudder pressure requirements change. Right rudder pressure becomes necessary for proper coordination and heading control. The high angle of attack, high torque, and pronounced P-factor create left-turning tendencies. If you do not apply right rudder, these tendencies will cause the airplane to turn to the left. You should refer to the ball of the turn coordinator to help determine the amount of rudder required.

Use right rudder pressure to compensate for torque and P-factor.

While you are maneuvering at critically slow airspeeds, you will get a sensation of insufficient control response. The controls feel "mushy," and it is necessary to use greater control movements for corrections than are normally required. The response of the airplane to control movements is also slow.

ALTITUDE AND AIRSPEED CONTROL

If you attempt to climb by applying back pressure during flight at critically slow airspeeds, you will not be successful. Instead, the airspeed will decrease, stall indications will occur, and the altitude will decrease.

If you lose altitude by lowering the nose, the airspeed will increase beyond acceptable limits. The correct procedure for regaining lost altitude is to apply power. When you do this, it will also be necessary to make a small increase in pitch attitude to maintain the desired airspeed. To lose altitude, reduce power and, at the same time, reduce pitch attitude slightly.

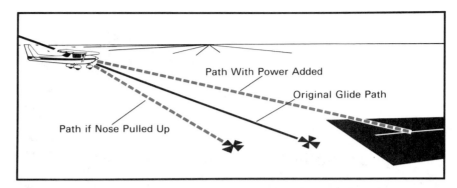

Figure 4-2. During final approach, if you apply control wheel back pressure in an attempt to extend the glide, the airspeed decreases and an even steeper glide angle is created. The correct procedure is to add power and adjust pitch to maintain the proper approach speed.

The approach-to-landing phase of flight gives a practical application of the relationship of power and airspeed. Assuming a stabilized approach, if the airplane appears to be low while on final approach at a constant airspeed, you must apply additional power and adjust pitch attitude as necessary. [Figure 4-2]

CLIMBS, DESCENTS, AND TURNS

When you are flying at critically slow airspeeds, altitude is controlled by power. To climb, add power; to descend, reduce power and adjust pitch attitude as necessary to maintain a constant airspeed. To execute turns at critically slow airspeeds, you must use a slightly different technique. As in any turn, part of the total lift force is diverted to make the airplane turn. For example, during a turn at normal cruise airspeed, you must apply slight control wheel back pressure to gain the extra vertical lift needed. This requirement results in a slight decrease in airspeed. However, during flight at critically slow airspeeds, the loss of airspeed brings the airplane closer to the stall. The steeper the turn, the greater the load factor and the higher the stall speed. Therefore, you should make shallow turns and add power to maintain sufficient airspeed to prevent a stall. Even when you apply full power, a stall may occur because you have exceeded the critical angle of attack while trying to maintain altitude.

USE OF FLAPS

Extend and retract flaps in small increments.

You will also practice maneuvering at critically slow airspeeds using flaps and landing gear, if the airplane has retractable gear. During practice, the instructor will tell you to lower the flaps. You should do this a small amount at a time. At each position, pause to adjust the attitude to correct airspeed, adjust power to maintain altitude, and retrim to relieve control wheel pressures.

Addition of flaps to the first position (10° to 15°) normally causes small changes in pitch attitude, power, and trim. However, with flaps extended beyond this amount, large changes may be required. When you extend the flaps completely, the pitch attitude change and power requirement usually are quite pronounced. With the wing flaps fully extended, drag is very high, and a large percentage of available power is required to maintain altitude. Full power will probably produce only a very slow rate of climb, if any.

RETURN TO CRUISE FLIGHT

To return to cruise airspeed from flight at critically slow airspeeds, first apply full power while maintaining a constant altitude, then raise the flaps slowly, one position at a time. This technique is recommended to allow the speed to increase gradually as you retract the flaps. [Figure 4-3]

Figure 4-3. According to the indicator on the left, the airplane may have a safe margin of airspeed with the flaps extended. However, the airspeed indicator on the right shows that sudden or complete retraction of the flaps at that speed may place the airplane near the stall speed in a no-flap condition.

CHECKLIST

After studying this section, you should have a basic understanding of:

✓ **Altitude and airspeed control** — How to use power and pitch to control the altitude and airspeed of the airplane when it is operated at critically slow airspeeds.

✓ **Climbs, descents, and turns** — How to establish and maintain a climb, descent, or turn while maintaining flight at critically slow airspeeds.

✓ **Recovery** — The procedures used to accelerate the airplane to straight-and-level flight.

POWER-OFF STALLS

Stalls are practiced to accomplish two main objectives. First, they enable you to become familiar with the stall warnings and handling characteristics of an airplane as it transitions from cruise to critically slow airspeeds and approaches a stall. Second, if you inadvertently enter a stall, you will be conditioned to recover promptly and effectively with a minimum loss of altitude.

CERTIFICATION REGULATIONS

FAR Part 23 prescribes the airworthiness standards for light airplanes. It contains the regulations pertaining to flight performance and handling characteristics, structure, powerplant, equipment, and operating limitations. Before a manufacturer can offer an airplane for sale, it must meet the specifications of this regulation, including flight testing and stall demonstrations. You should find the following points of particular interest:

1. You must be able to correct a roll or yaw up to the stall. This means that you must have effective use of the controls up to actual stall occurrence.
2. You must be able to prevent more than 15° of roll or 15° of yaw through normal use of controls during the recovery from a stall. In short, the controls must be effective during the recovery.
3. There must be a clear and distinct stall warning with the landing gear and flaps in any position you choose and in either straight or turning flight. The stall warning must begin between 5 and 10 knots before the stall occurs, continue into the stall, and end with the recovery. The acceptable stall warning can be buffeting or vibration of the airplane just prior to the actual stall or a visual or aural stall warning instrument.
4. If the airplane loses more than 100 feet or pitches more than 30° nose down during the stall demonstration, this information must be listed in the aircraft flight manual.

CAUSES OF THE STALL

Simply stated, a stall is caused by an excessive angle of attack, which causes the smooth airflow over the upper wing surface to break away, resulting in a loss of lift. However, the stall does not occur over the entire wing area at once. For example, consider a wing planform that begins to stall first at the wingtips and then spreads inward toward the root. This is an undesirable characteristic, since the disrupted airflow near the wingtip can reduce aileron effectiveness to such an extent that it may be

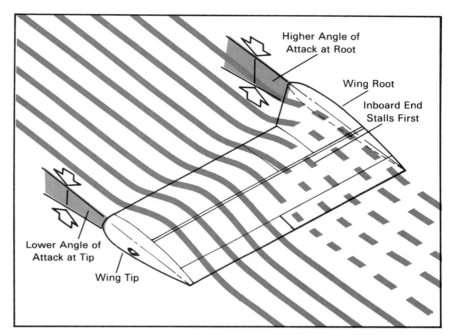

Figure 4-4. When wing twist is incorporated into the wing design, the wingtip has a lower angle of incidence than the wing root (usually two or three degrees). This results in the wingtip having a lower angle of attack than the root during the approach to a stall. Thus, the wingtip and ailerons will still be flying and providing positive control when the wing root has stalled.

impossible to control the airplane about its longitudinal axis. One method often used by airplane designers to prevent this problem is to incorporate a slight twist or washout in the wing. [Figure 4-4]

Another method sometimes used to assure positive control during the stall is installation of **stall strips**, which consist of two metal strips attached to the leading edge of each wing near the fuselage. These strips disrupt the airflow at high angles of attack, causing the wing area directly behind them to stall before the wingtips stall.

Remember, the airplane will stall whenever the critical angle of attack of the wing is exceeded. The stall can occur at any airspeed and in any flight attitude. The indicated airspeed at which the stall occurs varies with the airplane's weight, G-loading, and power and flap settings. The *Private Pilot Text* contains a complete discussion of the aerodynamics of stalls.

STALL PRACTICE

Practice stalls in an area away from other air traffic at an altitude that will allow you to recover from a stall at least 1,500 feet above the ground.

Before stall practice, as well as prior to other maneuvers, remember to make clearing turns to ensure there are no other airplanes in the area. If there are airplanes nearby, wait until they are well clear before performing the maneuver.

You will do the first stall from a power-off, wings-level glide, such as the one you use when you land the airplane. This is called a power-off stall. To enter the stall, apply carburetor heat (if required), reduce power to idle, apply full flaps (once a safe flap extension speed has been attained), establish a normal glide, and trim the airplane. Next, start to slow the airplane by applying back pressure on the control wheel.

Near the stall, the controls feel mushy and the engine and slipstream noises are reduced.

One objective of the maneuver is to gain a "feel" for the control pressures and responses as the airplane approaches the stall. As speed slows, the airplane's response to control pressures becomes slower, and it is necessary to use greater displacement of the controls to achieve the desired results. The feeling is sometimes called "mushy" or "soft," as compared to the more solid feel of the controls at cruise speed. As you approach the stall, there are other cues that tell you the airplane is slowing. For example, the engine sound decreases, as does the tone and intensity of the slipstream noise.

The stall warning begins 5 to 10 knots before the stall. The warning indications may be a light, buzzer, horn, buffeting, or any combination of these. One of the purposes of stall practice is to recognize the indications applicable to your airplane.

During the first demonstration, you will recover to straight-and-level flight after observing the first buffeting or decay of control effectiveness, and before the stall is fully developed. Approaching close to the stall, but not fully stalling, is referred to as performing an **imminent stall**. [Figure 4-5]

After you add power, move the carburetor heat control (if in use) to the COLD or OFF position. Normally, flaps are then retracted to an intermediate setting; however, the retraction procedures for stall recovery vary widely from one airplane to another. As the airplane accelerates, you should initiate a climb and continue to retract the remaining flaps.

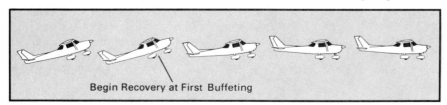
Begin Recovery at First Buffeting

Figure 4-5. Your first action to recover from a power-off stall is to decrease the angle of attack by releasing back pressure while simultaneously applying power. Move the throttle promptly and smoothly to obtain all available power. In addition, apply appropriate rudder pressure to center the ball of the turn coordinator.

Figure 4-6. During full-stall practice, the airplane may tend to roll to one side as the nose pitches down. If this occurs, use coordinated aileron and rudder pressures to level the wings at the same time you apply power and reestablish pitch attitude.

FULL STALLS

After practicing imminent stalls, you will learn to recover from full stalls. The initial setup of full-stall practice is exactly the same as for imminent stalls. The warnings of the stall are the same, but you will continue to increase back pressure beyond the point where you initiated recovery for the imminent stall. A full stall usually is evidenced by a high sink rate, uncontrollable nose-down pitching, and buffeting.

The recovery for the full stall is the same as for the imminent stall; release back pressure and simultaneously apply full power. Normally, you should retract the flaps to an intermediate setting. As the airspeed begins to increase following the recovery, readjust the pitch attitude gently and smoothly. [Figure 4-6]

SECONDARY STALL

The increase in stall speed which accompanies an increase in G-loading is an important consideration during stall recoveries. As the nose of the airplane is raised after stall recovery, you will be increasing the G-loading on the airplane. This causes a corresponding increase in stall speed. If the increase in stall speed exceeds the airspeed, the airplane will immediately enter a secondary stall. [Figure 4-7]

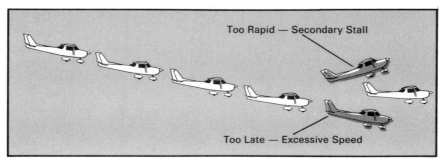

Too Rapid — Secondary Stall

Too Late — Excessive Speed

Figure 4-7. It is important for you to apply the correct amount of back pressure during stall recoveries. Applying back pressure too rapidly may result in a secondary stall, while not applying it rapidly enough may cause the airplane to build excessive airspeed and lose a significant amount of altitude.

TURNING FLIGHT STALLS

Once your instructor is satisfied that you can properly execute power-off stalls straight ahead, you will be asked to perform them during turning flight. The entry procedure is exactly the same as that used for stalls performed straight ahead, except your instructor will have you enter a turn using approximately 30° of bank. Initially, you normally begin with imminent stalls, then progress to full stalls.

Recovery, as with all stalls, begins by lowering the nose and applying full power. Then, bring the wings to a level flight attitude by coordinated use of the ailerons and rudder, and retract the flaps to an intermediate setting. As the airplane accelerates, begin a climb and retract the remaining flaps.

CHECKLIST

After studying this section, you should have a basic understanding of:

✓ **Stalls** — Why an airplane stalls and how the wing is designed to provide you with positive control throughout the stall entry and recovery.

✓ **Stall entry and recovery** — What the procedures are for entering and recovering from a stall.

✓ **Full and imminent stalls** — What the difference is between these two types of stalls and how to recognize each.

✓ **Secondary stalls** — What a secondary stall is and how to avoid one.

POWER-ON AND ACCELERATED STALLS

Once you have gained proficiency in power-off stalls, your instructor will demonstrate and allow you to practice power-on stalls. You will first practice power-on, imminent stalls; then you will proceed to full stalls from straight and turning flight. Once you are proficient in power-on stalls, your instructor will introduce the accelerated maneuver stall.

POWER-ON STALLS

The power-on, straight-ahead stall is the type most frequently encountered shortly after takeoff. This stall can occur if you attempt to lift the airplane from the runway at too slow an airspeed and apply excessive back pressure to the control wheel. This produces an extreme nose-high attitude and high angle of attack. This type of stall also can occur when you are flying at a low altitude over terrain which increases in elevation faster than the airplane is able to climb. The power-on, turning stall normally occurs during the departure turn following takeoff. This type of stall generally results from distractions that divert your attention from flying the airplane. During practice of these stalls, you should select an altitude that allows the recovery to be completed at an altitude of no less than 1,500 feet AGL.

STRAIGHT-AHEAD STALL

Although you will use a high power setting during this stall, do not enter it from a high airspeed. If you use a high airspeed, the pitch attitude you will encounter is extremely nose high. After you complete your clearing turns, reduce power and slow the airplane to near liftoff speed while maintaining a constant altitude. Then, add back pressure to increase the angle of attack, while simultaneously increasing power to the takeoff or recommended climb setting.

The power-on stall is entered near liftoff speed.

In order to maintain directional control and coordination, increase right rudder pressure continually as you increase the power and pitch attitude. Throughout the approach to the stall and the recovery, you should maintain coordinated flight.

INDICATIONS OF THE APPROACHING STALL

You should develop an awareness of the various indications of the approaching stall as the airspeed decreases. For example, the noise of the slipstream passing over the airplane and the engine noise level decrease

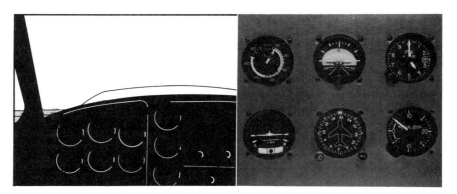

Figure 4-8. The pitch attitude in a power-on, straight-ahead stall resembles the visual relationship of the nose and horizon shown on the left. The instrument indications are pictured on the right. The angle created by the wingtips and the horizon can also provide a useful indication of the airplane's pitch attitude.

as the engine begins to labor during the climb. In addition, the flight controls feel mushy and soft. [Figure 4-8]

RECOVERY PROCEDURES

The procedures for recovery from the power-on stall are basically the same as for the power-off stall. Decrease the angle of attack while you simultaneously apply full available power (if you are not already at full power), and use coordinated aileron and rudder pressures to return the airplane to straight-and-level flight or establish a climb, as appropriate.

FULL STALLS

Maintain coordinated flight throughout stall entry and recovery.

After you become familiar with the characteristics of the power-on, imminent stall, you will begin practicing full stalls. You enter this type of stall in the same manner as the imminent stall. Clear the area and reduce power and airspeed. Just above liftoff speed, increase power to the recommended takeoff or climb power setting. Observe the indications of the approaching stall, maintain directional control, and continue to increase the angle of attack until the stall occurs. When the stall has developed fully, pronounced buffeting usually becomes evident and the nose normally pitches down, even though you hold full back pressure. There is a tendency for the airplane to pitch more steeply and rapidly and exhibit more right- or left-rolling tendencies in the full stall than in the imminent stall. However, by maintaining coordinated flight throughout the entry and recovery, you can minimize this rolling tendency. [Figure 4-9]

The main objective in stall recovery is to maintain positive and effective control of the airplane while losing minimum altitude. A common error made during stall recovery is using an excessive nose-down pitch attitude. The ideal recovery should be to a near-level attitude that results in minimum altitude loss and does not cause a secondary stall.

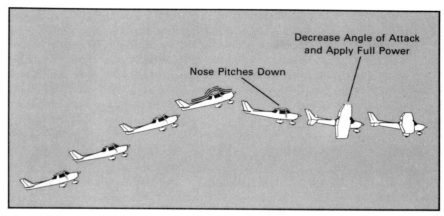

Figure 4-9. To recover from a power-on stall, decrease the angle of attack by releasing control wheel back pressure to lower the nose. You simultaneously add all available power and use the rudder and ailerons in a coordinated manner to return the airplane to straight-and-level flight or to establish a climb, as appropriate.

TURNING STALLS

The power-on turning stall is just a variation of the power-on, straight-ahead stall. After clearing the area, enter a power-on turning stall in the same way you enter a straight-ahead stall, but add a 20° banked turn to the left or right.

As you approach the stall, the angle of bank tends to steepen in a left turn and become shallower in a right turn. This occurs because of the tendency of torque and P-factor to roll the airplane to the left. When you practice stalls in each of these variations, you should try to identify the indications of the approaching stall and use coordinated ailerons and rudder throughout the entire maneuver.

The recovery is the same as for the power-on, straight-ahead stall. Lower the nose while simultaneously applying full power, then use coordinated ailerons and rudder pressures to return the airplane to straight-and-level flight or a climb, as appropriate.

ACCELERATED MANEUVER STALLS

After practicing power-on and power-off stalls from straight and turning flight, you will learn the accelerated maneuver stall. The term "accelerated" refers to a stall which occurs at a higher-than-normal airspeed because of an additional load factor. This increased load factor is normally induced during a steep turn.

To avoid extremely high structural loads, perform accelerated maneuver stalls only when you are operating below the airplane's maneuvering speed. Also, avoid abrupt pitch changes because of the high gyroscopic loads produced by the propeller. The stall speed increase during an

Accelerated stalls must be performed only when you are below maneuvering speed.

accelerated maneuver stall can be substantial. Stall speed is approximately equal to the one-G stall speed of the airplane multiplied by the square root of the load factor. For example, if you place the airplane in a 60° bank and maintain level flight, you are imposing a load factor of two G's. Since the square root of two is 1.4, the one-G stall speed is multiplied by 1.4 to obtain the two-G stall speed. Assuming the airplane used in this example has a one-G stall speed of 55 knots, placing it in a 60° bank will increase the stall speed to 78 knots ($\sqrt{2}$ = 1.4 x 55 = 78).

To begin the accelerated maneuver stall, check the area for other traffic by making clearing turns and select an entry altitude that allows you to complete the maneuver at an altitude no lower than 1,500 feet AGL. Then, while maintaining straight-and-level flight, reduce the airspeed of the airplane below its published maneuvering speed. Next, roll the airplane into a 45° level turn and firmly apply back elevator pressure to initiate a stall. Normally, you start your recovery at the first indication of a stall by releasing sufficient back pressure to eliminate all indications of the stall and simultaneously applying all available power. Finally, use coordinated ailerons and rudder pressure to return the airplane to straight-and-level flight.

SPINS

The airplane must be in a stalled condition before it can spin.

A spin can develop when one wing stalls before the other. When this happens, lift on the stalled wing is lost and it begins to drop. If the other wing is still producing some lift, the lifting forces are out of balance. This imbalance between the stalled wing and the flying wing leads to rotation approximately about the vertical axis. A **spin** can, therefore, be defined as an aggravated stall which results in autorotation. The key word for you to remember in this definition is "stall." In order for a spin to develop, a stall must occur first.

Since an airplane must be in a stalled condition before it will spin, the first thing you should do as you approach an inadvertent spin is try to recover from the stall before the spin develops. If your reaction is too slow and the spin develops, move the throttle to idle and retract the flaps if they are extended. Next, apply full rudder deflection opposite the direction of rotation. Just after the rudder reaches the stop, briskly position the control wheel forward of the neutral position to decrease the angle of attack (break the stall) and hold these control inputs. As the rotation stops, neutralize the rudder and smoothly apply back pressure to recover from the steep nose-down pitch attitude. During recovery from the dive, make sure you avoid excessive airspeed and high G-loadings. The recovery procedure can vary from airplane to airplane; therefore, be sure you are familiar with the spin recovery technique published in the pilot's operating handbook for the airplane you fly.

Most airplanes manufactured today are not required to demonstrate their ability to recover from a fully developed spin. Intentionally entering a spin in these airplanes can be extremely dangerous. However, if an airplane approved for spins is available, your instructor may demonstrate one for you. Keep in mind that, even when using an airplane approved for spins, recovery techniques vary. This is why you should never intentionally spin any airplane without an experienced instructor on board.

Never spin an airplane which has not been specifically approved for spins.

CHECKLIST

After studying the section, you should have a basic understanding of:

✓ **Entry and recovery procedures** — How to enter and recover from power-on stalls.

✓ **Rudder usage** — What the importance of the rudder is during the entry and recovery from power-on stalls.

✓ **Accelerated maneuver stalls** — What this type of stall is and how to enter and recover from it.

✓ **Spins** — Why an airplane spins and how to recover from a spin.

CONSTANT ALTITUDE TURNS

The constant altitude or steep turn is an excellent maneuver for developing coordination, planning, and precise airplane control. The following discussion applies primarily to constant altitude turns required for private pilot certification. This maneuver consists of a coordinated 360° turn performed at a bank angle of 40° to 50°. For simplicity, 45° banks are used in this text.

As in all training maneuvers, you must be aware of other traffic in the area. Therefore, before beginning the maneuver, make clearing turns to ensure the practice area is free of conflicting traffic. As you perform the maneuver, it is your responsibility to remain vigilant and avoid any traffic flying through the area.

To enter a constant altitude turn, stabilize the altitude, airspeed, and heading of the airplane. If you begin the maneuver from a stabilized condition, you can fly it more precisely. Use section lines or prominent land features to establish an entry heading and aid in orientation. As with most in-flight maneuvers, select an entry altitude that will allow the maneuver to be completed no lower than 1,500 feet AGL.

TURN ENTRY

Enter constant altitude turns at the speed recommended in the pilot's operating handbook. If no recommendation is given, use cruise speed or maneuvering speed, whichever is less. As you enter the turn, establish the bank at a moderate rate. If you roll the airplane into the bank too rapidly, you often will have difficulty establishing the pitch attitude necessary to maintain level flight.

As you establish the turn, increased power and back pressure are required.

Normally, you add power as the bank angle approaches 45°. Even when you apply power, the airspeed usually decreases and you must apply considerable back pressure to maintain altitude. You can use the trim to help relieve control wheel pressure in the turn, but you must remember to change the trim again as you complete the turn and roll out to straight-and-level flight.

VISUAL AND INSTRUMENT REFERENCES

As you roll into a constant altitude turn, establish the correct pitch and bank attitudes by referring to the natural horizon. Use the attitude indicator to confirm the correct attitudes. Once you are established in the

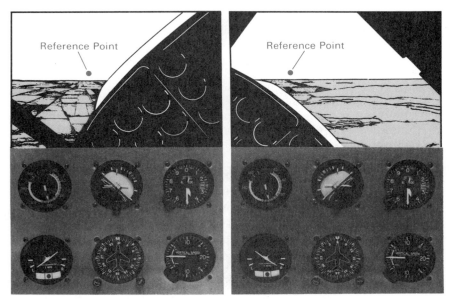

Figure 4-10. Here are the visual and instrument indications you will see when established in a level, constant altitude turn to the left and right. In a stable turn, the only instrument which shows a continual change is the heading indicator.

turn, maintain proper pitch and bank by referring to both the natural horizon and attitude indicator. Use the altimeter and vertical speed indicator to show when you must change pitch. [Figure 4-10]

ALTITUDE CONTROL

Altitude corrections in turns of 45° or more deserve special consideration. If you lose altitude because of a nose-low attitude, simply pulling back on the control wheel may not provide a satisfactory correction. The force created by back pressure on the control wheel raises the nose, but it also tightens the turn. This procedure simply increases the load on the airplane and does little to correct for altitude. The proper response is to reduce the angle of bank temporarily and simultaneously increase the pitch attitude. When you have made this correction, return to the desired angle of bank and apply slightly more back pressure than you used previously.

When you lose altitude in a constant altitude turn, decrease the angle of bank, increase pitch, then roll back into the turn.

ROLL-OUT TECHNIQUE

Perform the roll-out procedures for constant altitude turns in the same manner as those for medium bank turns. However, you should begin the roll-out approximately 20° before reaching the desired heading. Generally, less rudder pressure and aileron movement are required during the roll-in than during the roll-out. This is because the control pressures exerted during the roll-out must overcome the airplane's overbanking tendency.

The elevator (or stabilator) control pressures you use during the roll-out are the reverse of those used during the roll-in. As the bank decreases, you must decrease back pressure and pitch attitude gradually to avoid gaining altitude and to reduce power back to the cruise power setting.

When you gain proficiency in constant altitude turns in both directions, you will learn to perform them first in one direction, then in the other, with no hesitation between the turns. To accomplish this, you must apply back pressure during the first turn, reduce it during the roll-out, then reapply it as the angle of bank increases in the opposite direction.

OVERBANKING TENDENCY

When an airplane is in a level, constant altitude turn, **overbanking tendency** exists because the wing on the outside of the turn travels farther than the inside wing. Because it is traveling farther, the outside wing has a faster airflow over its surface. The higher airflow results in more lift on the outside wing. [Figure 4-11]

In addition, rudder pressure is required throughout the turn. The tail section, because of its distance aft of the center of gravity of the airplane, does not track in the same arc. Therefore, you need rudder pressure to streamline the fuselage in the arc of the turn.

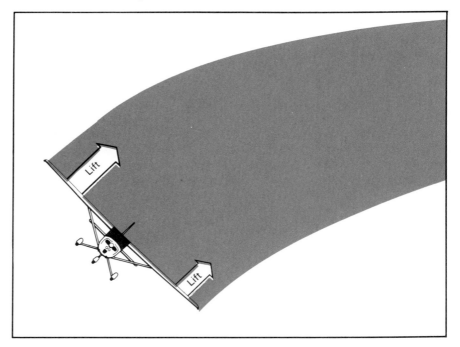

Figure 4-11. The increase in lift on the outside wing tends to increase bank. To counteract this tendency, you must apply slight aileron pressure opposite to the turn.

TORQUE AND P-FACTOR

You will notice less overbanking tendency in a right turn than in a left turn. This is due to torque and P-factor, which tend to roll the airplane to the left and work against the overbanking tendency in a right turn. However, these factors increase the overbanking tendency during left turns.

CHECKLIST _____

After studying this section, you should have a basic understanding of:

✓ **Entry and recovery procedures** — How to enter and recover from a constant altitude turn.

✓ **Altitude recovery** — The correct procedure to use in the event altitude is lost in a constant altitude turn.

✓ **Overbanking tendencies, torque, and P-factor** — How these affect the airplane when it is established in a turn, as well as during turn entry and recovery, and how to compensate for them.

CHAPTER 5

GROUND REFERENCE MANEUVERS

INTRODUCTION

As you become more comfortable with the airplane, you will begin to practice exercises that require you to divide your attention between flying the airplane and following a prescribed path over the ground. The maneuvers described in this chapter are rectangular courses, S-turns, and turns around a point. They are collectively called ground reference maneuvers. To some degree, you execute these maneuvers each time you fly in the traffic pattern or proceed to and from the practice area. Practicing them will assist you in maneuvering the airplane more precisely during all phases of flight.

DETERMINING WIND

You should estimate the wind's speed and direction before you begin any ground reference maneuver.

You can prepare for flying ground reference maneuvers by determining the direction of the wind before you leave the airport. Then, verify the direction and velocity of the wind as you approach the practice area. [Figure 5-1]

Another method you can employ to determine wind direction is to fly a 360° constant airspeed, constant bank turn. Your path over the ground will provide valuable information about the wind. [Figure 5-2]

RECTANGULAR COURSE

The rectangular course is very similar to the standard traffic pattern.

As you fly a rectangular course, you will quickly notice its similarity to the traffic pattern. In fact, this maneuver helps you develop the skills needed to fly a uniform traffic pattern, because it requires you to compensate for the effects of wind.

The instructor normally selects a field well away from other traffic and populated areas with sides not more than one mile nor less than one-half mile in length. These dimensions are rough guidelines, but the shape should be square or rectangular within the approximate limits given. The maneuver is flown at an altitude of approximately 600 to 1,000 feet above ground level. The bank angle in the turning portions of the pattern should not exceed 45°.

Figure 5-1. The runway in use, wind sock indication, and movement of smoke or dust are valuable indications of wind direction. Wind also produces advancing wave patterns on water and grain fields, and leans rows of trees away from the wind.

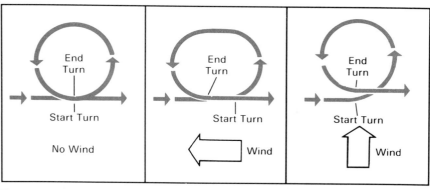

Figure 5-2. If an airplane turns at a constant speed and angle of bank in a calm wind condition, as shown on the left, the track over the ground is circular and the airplane completes the turn over the point where it began. In a headwind, as shown in the center, the turn is completed on the original track, but behind the point where it was started. In a direct crosswind, as shown on the right, you complete the turn abreast of, but on the downwind side of, the point where you started.

This maneuver requires you to combine several flight techniques. First, you may need to use varying crab angles throughout the straight flight segments. Second, you must track an imaginary line parallel to a fixed line. Third, you need to plan ahead and use different angles of bank in order to roll out of the turns at the proper distance from the field boundary. Finally, you must maintain a constant altitude throughout the maneuver. [Figure 5-3]

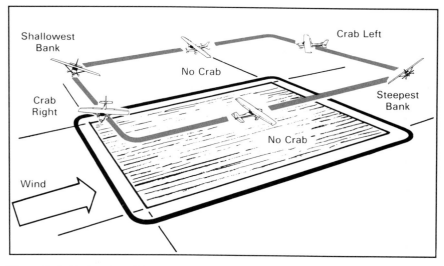

Figure 5-3. Notice that this pattern has two legs in which no crab angle is needed, since the airplane will have either a direct headwind or tailwind. It also has two legs which require crab angles in different directions. The bank angles required to make the turns symmetrical are functions of the airplane's groundspeed.

The flight path should not be directly over the edges of the field, but far enough away so the boundaries can be observed as you look out the side windows of the airplane. If you attempt to fly over the edges of the field, the required turns will be too steep or the maneuver will result in an oval-shaped course. The closer the track of the airplane is to the edges of the field, the steeper the bank required. Typically, the distance from the field boundary will be approximately one-quarter to one-half mile.

Start each turn as you arrive abeam each corner and roll out equidistant from the next side.

This maneuver may be entered from any direction. For the purposes of this discussion, though, assume that you enter the maneuver downwind. To begin, fly the airplane parallel to the field until you approach the corner. Start a turn at the exact time the airplane is abeam the corner. As you complete the turn, the airplane should be following a ground track that is parallel to and equidistant from the next side of the field. In determining the amount of bank to use, you will discover it to be a function of the airplane's groundspeed; the greater the groundspeed, the greater the angle of bank required. As you proceed through the first turn, your groundspeed decreases. Therefore, you will gradually decrease the bank to maintain your distance from the field. In addition, you will need to turn more than 90°, since a crab is usually required on the crosswind leg. Continue around the field, adjusting bank and crab angles as required to maintain a constant distance. After several circuits around the field, you may be asked to reverse your direction of flight.

The complexity of the rectangular course maneuver is increased when the wind blows across the course diagonally. In this situation, use a crab on all four legs. Practice this maneuver until you can fly correct ground tracks at the specified altitudes and distances. You may also be requested to alternately glide on a simulated final approach leg and climb back to the simulated traffic pattern altitude. This provides more realistic practice of an approach and climbout from an airport.

S-TURNS ACROSS A ROAD

As you discovered when flying the rectangular course, the angle of bank required during a symmetrical turn varies with the airplane's groundspeed. S-turns across a road are designed to help you further develop this skill.

Normally, your instructor will select a straight ground reference line or a road that lies perpendicular to the wind. The objective on this maneuver is to fly two perfect half-circles of equal size on opposite sides of the road at a constant altitude. As with most ground reference maneuvers, you enter the S-turn on a downwind heading at an altitude of approximately 600 to 1,000 feet AGL. The maximum bank for this maneuver also should be limited to 45°. As you cross the road, roll immediately into a bank. Since the airplane is flying downwind, it is at its highest groundspeed, so the bank angle is the steepest you will use throughout the

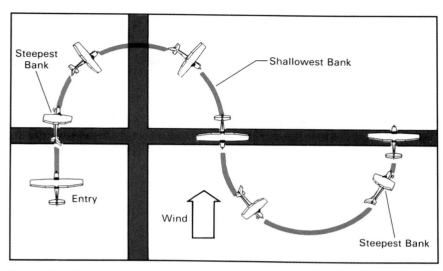

Figure 5-4. The shallowest angle of bank occurs just before and after the airplane crosses the road into the wind. The steepest bank occurs just before and after the airplane crosses the road downwind.

maneuver. As you continue through the turn, gradually reduce the bank to trace a symmetrical half circle. Time the roll-out so the airplane is rolled level, headed directly upwind, and is perpendicular to the road just as you cross it. [Figure 5-4]

At the completion of the first 180° of turn, the airplane should recross the road, then smoothly and gradually roll into a turn in the opposite direction. Since the airplane is headed upwind, this portion of the maneuver has the slowest groundspeed and requires the shallowest bank. Steepen the bank gradually throughout the turn to continue tracing a half-circle the same shape and size as the one on the opposite side of the road. You attain the steepest bank just before roll-out as you reach the road. The "S" is completed as the airplane crosses the road on a perpendicular flight path with the wings level.

TURNS AROUND A POINT

The final ground reference maneuver is called turns around a point. This maneuver further refines your skills in making constant radius turns around an object on the ground while maintaining a constant altitude.

Do not confuse the techniques for performing turns around a point with the steep turns performed át altitude with a constant angle of bank. This maneuver requires you to perform constant radius turns around a pre-selected point on the ground. Your objective is to maintain a constant altitude and roll out on the initial entry heading after completing the number of turns specified by your instructor. The maneuver is flown at an altitude of 600 to 1,000 feet AGL, and the bank is normally limited to a maximum of 45°.

Select a reference point that is prominent and easily distinguished, yet small enough to establish a definite location. It should be in the center of an area away from livestock, buildings, or concentrations of people on the ground. This prevents annoyance and undue hazard. You should also select an area that affords the opportunity for a safe emergency landing.

You can use trees, isolated haystacks, or other small landmarks, but they are not as effective as the intersections of roads or fence lines. The latter items are more effective, because the wing may momentarily block your view of the reference point during the maneuver. By selecting a road or fence line intersection, you can mentally project these lines to their logical intersection and maintain your orientation.

The easiest way to enter this maneuver is to fly downwind at a distance from the point equal to the radius of the desired turn. As you arrive exactly abeam the selected point, enter a 45° bank turn toward the side on which your reference point is located. Then, carefully plan the track over the ground and vary the bank, as necessary, to maintain that track. [Figure 5-5]

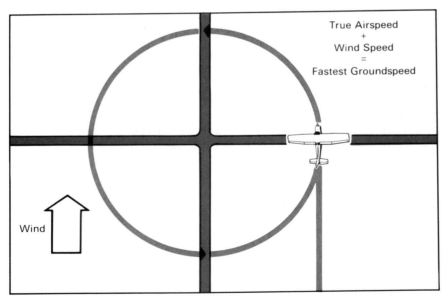

True Airspeed
+
Wind Speed
=
Fastest Groundspeed

Wind

Figure 5-5. Decrease the bank continuously throughout the first 180° of turn until it reaches a minimum value (normally at or near level flight) as the airplane crosses the road into the wind. Throughout the next 180° of turn, steadily increase the angle of bank to its maximum value.

As you gain experience, you will practice turns around a point in both directions. Additionally, you should practice entering the maneuver at any point. Remember that the angle of bank at any given point is dependent on the radius of the circle being flown, the wind velocity, and the groundspeed. When you enter the maneuver at a point other than directly downwind, you must carefully select the angle of bank and the radius of the turn in terms of wind velocity and groundspeed. Also, you normally limit your maximum angle of bank to 45°, which occurs when the airplane is flying directly downwind.

CHECKLIST _____

After studying this section, you should have a basic understanding of:

✓ **Rectangular course** — What the objectives of this maneuver are, including the correct use of crab angles and the proper method for making symmetrical turns at each corner of the maneuver.

✓ **S-turns across a road** — How this maneuver is flown, and when the angle of bank is at its steepest and shallowest points.

✓ **Turns around a point** — What the purpose of this maneuver is, including an understanding of when to increase the angle of bank and when to decrease it.

MAXIMUM PERFORMANCE TAKEOFFS AND LANDINGS

CHAPTER 6

INTRODUCTION

During flight training, you typically learn to fly at airports with relatively long, paved runways. However, not all airports have long runways, and many runways are made of dirt, grass, or sod. It is important that you learn how to perform short-field and soft-field takeoffs, climbs, approaches, and landings. These maneuvers, also referred to as maximum performance takeoffs and landings, are designed to allow you to operate safely into and out of unimproved airports.

This chapter presents, in general terms, the techniques you will use to accomplish each maneuver. However, you should understand that these techniques may vary for any given model of airplane. Therefore, be sure to consult your pilot's operating handbook for the specific procedures applicable to your airplane.

Obstacle clearance, best angle-of-climb, and best rate-of-climb are three important speeds used during the initial climb.

Before presenting the techniques you will use in maximum performance takeoffs and landings, let's review some important terms. The **best angle-of-climb** speed provides the greatest altitude gain for a given distance over the ground. Many manufacturers also specify an **obstacle clearance** speed. This speed is used immediately after lift-off when the airplane is in the takeoff configuration and you must clear an obstacle located in the departure path.

Typically, you use the best angle-of-climb speed or the obstacle clearance speed, as appropriate to your airplane, until all obstacles in the takeoff path have been cleared. Next, you accelerate to the **best rate-of-climb** speed. This speed provides the greatest gain in altitude in a given period of time. Since optimum performance is achieved by maintaining each speed precisely, you should make every effort to hold the best angle-of-climb, obstacle clearance, and best rate-of-climb speeds as precisely as possible.

SHORT-FIELD TAKEOFF AND CLIMB

During short-field practice sessions it is usually assumed that, in addition to a short runway, there is an obstruction that you must clear on each end of the runway. The obstructions are considered to be approximately 50 feet in height. [Figure 6-1]

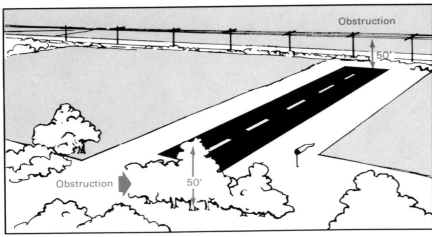

Figure 6-1. Trees and powerlines are common types of obstructions. However, during flight training, your instructor will usually simulate the existence of obstacles if none are present.

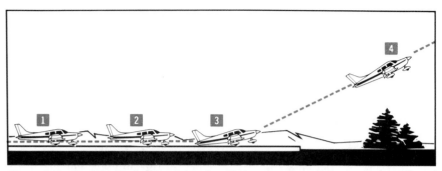

Figure 6-2. The initial takeoff roll involves little or no use of elevator (or stabilator) control beyond permitting it to assume a neutral position (position 1). As you reach the recommended rotation speed (position 2), apply prompt, positive back pressure to establish the proper takeoff attitude (position 3). Hold this attitude until the best angle-of-climb speed (or obstacle clearance speed) is established, then maintain this speed until the obstacle is cleared (position 4).

The pretakeoff checklist is the same as that used for normal takeoff procedures, except that you set the flaps as recommended by the airplane manufacturer. The recommended flap setting varies between airplanes and can range from no flaps to approximately one-half flaps.

Initiate the short-field takeoff by taxiing into position as close as possible to the end of the runway. Hold the brakes, apply full power, and then release the brakes. This procedure enables you to determine that the engine is functioning properly before you take off from a field where power availability is critical. As you begin the takeoff roll, maintain directional control with rudder pressure. A running, turning takeoff is not recommended, especially at high speeds, because this technique does not permit stabilization of fuel levels in the tanks of some airplanes. [Figure 6-2]

Check to determine that the engine is functioning properly before you release the brakes for takeoff.

Take care to avoid raising the nose prior to the recommended rotation speed. A premature nose-high attitude during the takeoff ground run produces more drag and causes a longer takeoff roll. After you have cleared the obstacle, lower the nose and accelerate to the best rate-of-climb speed. If you used flaps, retract them only after you have cleared the obstacle, established the best rate-of-climb speed, and climbed to a safe altitude.

SHORT-FIELD LANDING

During short-field landing practice, assume you are making the approach and landing over a 50-foot obstacle. Perform the landing from a full-flap stabilized approach and execute the touchdown with power off. By incorporating this technique, you can maneuver the airplane safely and accurately over the obstacle to a landing touchdown at the slowest possible groundspeed, producing the shortest possible ground roll.

The early part of the approach on the downwind leg and through the turn to base leg is very similar to a normal approach. You may extend approximately one-third of the available flaps during the latter portion of the downwind leg, two-thirds on base, and the remaining flaps on final approach, while progressively reducing the airspeed. Use the trim to remove control pressure.

FINAL APPROACH

The final approach path used for a short-field landing is somewhat steeper than the one used for a normal approach. It allows you to clear an obstacle located near the approach end of the runway. The use of full flaps during the approach allows a descent at a steeper angle without an increase in airspeed. This results in a overall decrease in the distance required to bring the airplane to a full stop. [Figure 6-3]

LANDING FLARE AND TOUCHDOWN

During the landing flare, reduce power smoothly to idle and allow the airplane to touch down in a full-stall attitude. When the airplane is firmly on the runway, lower the nose and apply the brakes, as necessary, to further shorten the landing roll. As your training progresses, your goal will be to touch down beyond and within 200 feet of a point specified by your instructor.

SOFT-FIELD TAKEOFF

The objective of the soft-field takeoff is to transfer the weight of the airplane from the landing gear to the wings as quickly and smoothly as possible. The soft-field takeoff procedure requires you to accelerate the airplane in a nose-high attitude, keeping the nosewheel clear of the surface during most of the takeoff ground run. This technique keeps the nosewheel from sinking into the soft runway surface and allows the airplane to become airborne as soon as possible.

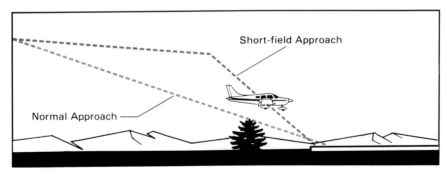

Figure 6-3. Two types of approach paths are shown here: the normal approach and the short-field approach. Notice when an obstacle is present how the short-field approach allows you to descend at a steeper angle and touch down closer to the end of the runway.

PRETAKEOFF CONSIDERATIONS

You actually begin the soft-field takeoff procedure during the taxi phase of the operation. If the taxi area is soft, you should use full-up elevator (or stabilator) deflection with a slight amount of power to help keep the airplane moving. This technique transfers some of the weight of the airplane from the nosewheel to the main wheels, resulting in lower power requirements and greater ease in taxiing. If practical, the pretakeoff check should be completed on a paved or firm-surfaced portion of the airport. This helps avoid propeller damage and the possibility of becoming stuck. After you complete the pretakeoff checklist, clear the approach and departure areas and the traffic pattern prior to taxiing onto the runway. In this manner, when there is no conflicting traffic, you can transition the airplane from the taxi phase to the takeoff roll without stopping. This technique allows the airplane to maintain momentum as you taxi over the soft surface.

> While taxiing, maintain full back pressure on the control wheel.

USE OF RUDDER

As you taxi the airplane into position for takeoff and align it with the center of the runway, apply the remaining power smoothly and maintain full back pressure on the control wheel. When you apply takeoff power, you may need right rudder pressure to maintain directional control due to the effects of torque, P-factor, and spiraling slipstream. When the nosewheel is clear of the runway surface, nosewheel steering becomes ineffective. However, due to the increasing air flow, the rudder becomes sufficiently effective for maintaining directional control.

PITCH CONTROL

As you apply power and initiate the takeoff roll, maintain full back pressure to raise the nosewheel from the soft surface. As you increase speed and the elevator (or stabilator) becomes more effective, you will need to reduce back pressure slightly. If you do not reduce back pressure, the airplane may assume an extremely nose-high attitude, which can cause the tail skid to come in contact with the runway. [Figure 6-4]

> It is important to raise the nosewheel clear of the runway as soon as practical, but do not allow the tail to come in contact with the ground.

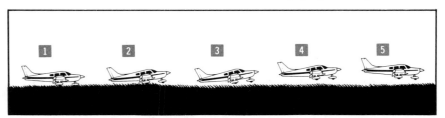

Figure 6-4. If you establish the proper pitch attitude during acceleration (position 1), the nosewheel will be clear of the surface during much of the ground run (position 2), and the airplane will lift off at or slightly below the power-off stall speed (position 3). After liftoff, reduce the pitch attitude gradually to level flight (position 4), allowing the airplane to accelerate within ground effect to the normal climb airspeed (position 5).

GROUND EFFECT

During the takeoff, you will be aided by a phenomenon called **ground effect**. This is an increase in lift during flight, which is due primarily to the redirection of the air between the wings of the airplane and the surface of the earth. Ground effect allows the airplane to sustain flight at very low airspeeds and altitudes. However, this phenomenon is limited to a height above the ground which is about equal to the airplane's wingspan. For example, if the wingspan of the airplane is 40 feet, ground effect ends at approximately 40 feet above ground level. Since the intensity of ground effect decreases with altitude, you should fly the airplane as low as safety will permit until you have achieved the best angle-of-climb airspeed. Your *Private Pilot Manual* contains a complete discussion on this topic.

LIFTOFF AND FLAP RETRACTION

Be sure to accelerate to the best angle-of-climb speed before climbing out of ground effect.

As the airplane lifts from the runway surface, reduce back pressure to achieve a level flight attitude. You must then accelerate the airplane in level flight, within ground effect, to the best angle-of-climb airspeed before starting a climb. Do not retract the flaps, since the resultant loss of lift may cause the airplane to settle back onto the runway.

On a rough surface, it is possible for the airplane to skip or bounce into the air before its full weight can be supported aerodynamically. Therefore, it is important to hold the pitch attitude as constant as possible (an important application of maneuvering at critically slow airspeeds). If you permit the nose to lower after a bounce, it may cause the nosewheel to strike the ground with resulting damage. On the other hand, sharply increasing the pitch attitude after a bounce may cause the airplane to stall.

OBSERVATION OF PROPER AIRSPEEDS

Throughout the takeoff procedure, observe the proper airspeeds and plan the necessary climb segments accordingly. After the airplane is airborne, accelerate to the best angle-of-climb speed as quickly as possible. At this point, you may begin your climb out of ground effect. Once all obstacles are cleared, accelerate to the best rate-of-climb speed and continue the climb. You should retract the flaps once you have attained a safe altitude and airspeed.

SOFT-FIELD LANDING

Hold the nose clear of the runway as long as possible.

Conduct the soft-field landing from a normal full-flap approach. Touch down with a high angle of attack while applying necessary power for a soft touchdown. The objective is to ease the weight of the airplane from the wings to the main wheels as gently and slowly as possible while keeping the nosewheel clear of the runway. If you execute the landing properly, the total weight of the airplane rests on the main wheels with the nosewheel free of the soft surface during most of the landing roll. This technique prevents the nosewheel from sinking into the soft surface and reduces the possibility of an abrupt stop during the landing roll.

PITCH AND POWER CONTROL DURING LANDING

Proper pitch and power control are important during the entire approach and landing, but become most critical during the landing flare and touchdown segments. Change the pitch smoothly from an approach to a touchdown attitude. Normally, you will maintain a small amount of power during the touchdown to facilitate a nose-high, soft touchdown. The amount of power required varies with weight and density altitude. When you maintain power, the slipstream flow over the empennage makes the elevator (or stabilator) more effective. As the airspeed decreases on the roll-out, the slipstream becomes less effective. Allow the nosewheel to contact the runway surface gradually and smoothly.

CHECKLIST ─────────────────────────

After studying this section, you should have a basic understanding of:

✓ **Climb speeds** — When best angle-of-climb, obstacle clearance climb, and best rate-of-climb speeds are used.

✓ **Short-field takeoff** — What the procedures are to ensure a takeoff using the least amount of runway.

✓ **Short-field landing** — How to execute the short-field landing.

✓ **Soft-field takeoff** — How to execute a takeoff when departing an airport with unimproved runways and why these procedures are necessary.

✓ **Soft-field landing** — How to land on unimproved runways and why the nosewheel is held clear of the runway.

ATTITUDE INSTRUMENT AND NIGHT FLYING

CHAPTER 7

INTRODUCTION

So far in your training, you have been using the natural horizon to determine the pitch and bank attitude of the airplane. Section A of this chapter expands on this fundamental skill. It provides you with an introduction to the skills required to fly an airplane when the natural horizon is not visible. In Section B, you will be introduced to the differences between night flight and daylight operations. In addition, you will see how it enhances flight safety to be able to use the flight instruments effectively at night.

SECTION A

ATTITUDE INSTRUMENT FLYING

Attitude instrument flying is a fundamental method for controlling an airplane by reference to instruments. It is based on an understanding of the flight instruments and systems. This knowledge will help you develop the skills required to interpret and translate the information presented by the instruments into precise airplane control. Instrument scanning (or cross-check), instrument interpretation, and airplane control are the three fundamental skills involved in all instrument flight maneuvers. You develop these skills individually, then integrate them into coordinated, positive control responses.

Instrument training is required for private pilot certification. The purpose of this is not to qualify you to fly in instrument weather conditions. Rather, this training will allow you to get out of instrument conditions quickly and safely in case of an unintentional encounter. Even after you have attained reasonable skill in performing the basic attitude instrument maneuvers and recoveries from critical or unusual flight attitudes, you should never undertake flight in instrument conditions until you are appropriately rated. However, these newly acquired skills will serve as a good foundation for further instrument training and the eventual addition of an instrument rating.

FLIGHT INSTRUMENTS

During flight by instrument references, use the attitude indicator as a substitute for the natural horizon.

In visual flight, airplane attitude is usually determined by reference to the earth's horizon. For example, pitch attitude normally is determined by the position of the airplane's nose in relation to the natural horizon, while the wingtips provide information concerning bank. However, when you are flying in visual conditions, you do not determine the airplane's altitude by looking down at the ground and estimating the height, but by reference to the altimeter. You approximate the speed of the airplane by the sound of the slipstream, but you determine it more precisely through use of the airspeed indicator. You can estimate the direction of flight in relation to the sun's position, but it is easier to use the heading indicator. During flight by instrument references, the natural horizon is replaced by the attitude indicator, and the remaining instruments have the same function as during visual flight. The general information provided by the attitude indicator is correlated with the specific information gained from the altimeter, vertical speed indicator, heading indicator, turn coordinator, and airspeed indicator.

SCANNING

Scanning is the term applied to the continuous systematic cross-check of flight instruments. The actual technique may vary somewhat, depending on individual differences, various maneuvers, and variations in airplane equipment, as well as your experience and proficiency level. [Figure 7-1]

At first, you may have a tendency to scan rapidly, looking directly at the instruments without knowing exactly what information you are seeking. However, with familiarity and practice, the instrument scan reveals definite trends during specific flight conditions. These trends will help you control the airplane as it makes a transition from one flight condition to another. You also learn that, during some phases of flight, the instrument scan must be more rapid than at other times.

Throughout our lifetimes, most of us have learned to apply full concentration to a single task to perform it well. However, this tendency causes several errors that you can eliminate through awareness.

If you apply your full concentration to a single instrument, you will encounter a problem called **fixation**. This results from a natural human inclination to observe a specific instrument carefully and accurately, often to the exclusion of other instruments. Fixation on a single instrument usually results in poor control. For example, while performing a turn, you may have a tendency to watch only the turn coordinator instead of including other instruments in your cross-check. This fixation on the turn coordinator often leads to a loss of altitude through poor pitch and bank control. You should look at each instrument only long enough to understand the information it presents, then continue on to the next one.

Figure 7-1. In most situations, the scan pattern includes the attitude indicator between the scan of each of the other instruments. A typical scan might progress as follows: attitude indicator — altimeter — attitude indicator — VSI — attitude indicator — heading indicator — attitude indicator, and so on.

Similarly, you may find yourself placing too much **emphasis** on a single instrument, instead of relying on a combination of instruments necessary for airplane performance information. This differs from fixation in that you are using other instruments, but are giving too much attention to a particular one.

During performance of a maneuver, you may sometimes fail to anticipate significant instrument indications following attitude changes. For example, during leveloff from a climb or descent, you may concentrate on pitch control, while forgetting about heading or roll information. This error, called **omission**, results in erratic control of heading and bank.

In spite of these common errors, most pilots can adapt well to flight by instrument reference after instruction and practice. You may find that you can control the airplane more easily and precisely by instruments. In fact, during visual flight, beginning pilots sometimes rely too heavily on instrument references when they should rely more on outside visual references and watch for other air traffic.

INSTRUMENT INTERPRETATION

To fly effectively by instrument reference, you should understand each instrument's operating principles and limitations. In addition, you need to know what each instrument reveals about the airplane's performance. Each flight maneuver involves the use of combinations of instruments that you must read and interpret in order to control the airplane. For example, if you want to control pitch attitude, use the attitude indicator, airspeed indicator, altimeter, and vertical speed indicator. To control bank attitude, use the attitude indicator, turn coordinator, and heading indicator. To determine both pitch and bank attitude by instrument reference, you must include all of the flight instruments in your scan.

To control an airplane by reference to instruments, you must continue perfecting the techniques of proper pitch, bank, and power control that you practiced during flight by visual reference. Maintain a light touch on the controls and trim off any control pressures once the airplane has stabilized in a particular attitude. Abrupt and erratic airplane movement and pilot fatigue result when light control pressures and correct use of trim are not used.

SENSORY PERCEPTIONS

During instrument flight, you must disregard your sense of balance in favor of what your flight instruments indicate.

A human being's ability to maintain equilibrium depends primarily on three senses—the sense of sight, the sense of changing position which originates in the balance organs of the inner ear, and the postural sense (kinesthesia) which includes sensations of touch, pressure, and tension on muscles, joints, and tendons. When flying under visual conditions, your orientation is maintained by using these senses. The primary sense is sight, which uses the natural horizon of the earth as a reference. However, during instrument flight, you must use the indications of your flight instruments to maintain your orientation with the earth.

During instrument flight, some of the sensations from the inner ear and postural sense tend to send conflicting information to the brain. Confusion results when the brain is unable to interpret whether the pressure and tension of the muscles is a result of gravity or of load factors induced during maneuvering. Therefore, you must learn to trust your instruments and react accordingly.

STRAIGHT-AND-LEVEL FLIGHT

To maintain accurate straight-and-level flight by instrument reference, you must learn to control the pitch and bank of the airplane through interpretation of the flight instruments. The following discussion of airplane control and flight instruments outlines the proper use and interpretation of the instrument indications as they relate to straight-and-level flight.

PITCH CONTROL

At a constant airspeed and power setting, there is only one specific pitch attitude which will maintain level flight. The instruments used to maintain pitch control are the attitude indicator, airspeed indicator, altimeter, and vertical speed indicator. Any change in the pitching motion of the airplane registers a change on these instruments in direct proportion to the magnitude of the change. [Figure 7-2]

When airspeed and power are held constant, pitch is used to maintain altitude.

Figure 7-2. As you enter a climb, the nose of the miniature airplane rises above the horizon bar of the attitude indicator. This causes a decrease in airspeed, an increase in altitude, and a positive rate-of-climb indication.

A pitch change to a nose-down attitude causes the miniature airplane on the attitude indicator to move below the horizon bar. In addition, an increase in airspeed, a decrease in altitude, and an indication of a descent on the vertical speed indicator are displayed on the flight instruments. Now let's take a closer look at the individual flight instruments.

ATTITUDE INDICATOR

The attitude indicator is the only instrument which indicates both pitch and bank attitude.

The attitude indicator is the only instrument which provides a pictorial display of the airplane's overall attitude. During instrument flight, all changes in pitch and bank are made by reference to this instrument. The other instruments are used to indicate when a change in attitude is required. [Figure 7-3]

During instrument flight, your instructor will demonstrate the relationship between the miniature airplane and the horizon bar during pitch changes. The displacement between the miniature airplane and the horizon bar on the attitude indicator appears to be much smaller than displacement of the actual airplane's nose in relation to the natural horizon. Therefore, you should use light control pressures and make the required attitude changes slowly and smoothly.

When practicing pitch control using the attitude indicator, you should initially restrict the displacement of the horizon bar to a one-half bar width up or down, progressing later to a full bar width. Use greater displacement only when large attitude changes are required. The control pressures necessary to make pitch changes vary in different airplanes. However, you cannot feel control pressure changes if you have a tight grip on the control wheel. If you maintain light pressures and retrim the

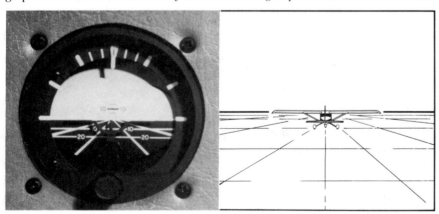

Figure 7-3. The attitude indicator shown here represents an airplane in straight-and-level flight. You determine pitch attitude by comparing the nose of the miniature airplane to the horizon bar or to the pitch indexes located on the face of the instrument. You can also determine bank by comparing the wings of the miniature airplane to the horizon bar or by comparing the bank pointer to the indexes located to each side.

airplane after it is stabilized in a new attitude, the result will be smooth and precise attitude control.

ALTIMETER

At a constant airspeed and power setting, altitude is controlled by pitch. The altimeter provides an indication of pitch attitude. Since the altitude should remain constant when the airplane is in level flight, any deviation from the desired altitude indicates the need for a pitch change. Obviously, if the altitude is increasing, the nose must be lowered. The rate of movement of the altimeter needle is as important as its direction of movement in maintaining level flight. Large pitch attitude deviations from level flight result in rapid altitude changes; slight pitch deviations produce much slower changes in the altimeter needle movement. Remember to make all adjustments to pitch by using the attitude indicator.

Altitude Correction Rules

A common rule for altitude corrections of less than 100 feet is to use a one-half bar width adjustment on the attitude indicator. For corrections in excess of 100 feet, use a full bar width correction. As you establish these corrections, observe the rate of altitude change on the vertical speed indicator and the altimeter.

If the deviation from the desired altitude is less than 100 feet, you can make the attitude adjustment you need to return to the correct altitude without changing the power setting. However, if the deviation from the desired altitude is greater than 100 feet, you should make a change in power setting and an appropriate trim adjustment.

VERTICAL SPEED INDICATOR

The normal function of the vertical speed indicator is to help you establish and maintain a desired rate of climb or descent. Due to the design of the instrument, there is a lag of approximately six to nine seconds before the correct rate of change is registered. Even though this lag exists, you may use the vertical speed indicator as a trend instrument for maintaining a desired pitch attitude. As a trend instrument, it indicates the direction of pitch change almost instantaneously.

If the needle deviates from the zero position, the instrument is indicating that the pitch is changing. Apply corrective pressures while referring to the attitude indicator. This pressure will stop the needle movement and place the airplane in a level attitude again. However, you should not try to return the needle to zero, since the lag in the vertical speed indicator will cause a tendency to overcontrol. Instead, after you have made a pitch correction to return to level flight, you should make an additional slight pitch correction to return to the desired altitude. Your judgment

For small adjustments in altitude, use a vertical speed equal to approximately twice the desired altitude change.

and experience in a particular airplane dictate the rate of altitude correction. As a guide, adjust the miniature airplane on the attitude indicator to produce a rate of change which is double the amount of altitude deviation, and use power as necessary. For example, if an airplane is 100 feet below the desired altitude, select a climb rate of 200 f.p.m. Estimate the initial amount of pitch change required to stop the descent and climb at 200 f.p.m. Hold it constant until the vertical speed indicator displays an accurate rate, then adjust it as necessary.

AIRSPEED INDICATOR

The airspeed indicator will also indicate pitch attitude. If you establish a constant pitch attitude and power setting and permit the airplane to stabilize, the airspeed remains constant. As you raise the pitch attitude, the airspeed decreases slightly. On the other hand, as you lower the pitch attitude, the airspeed increases somewhat.

A rapid change in airspeed indicates that a large pitch change has occurred; you should apply smooth control pressure in the opposite direction. Again, however, look at the attitude indicator to note the amount of pitch change caused by control pressure. This will help you avoid overcontrolling the airplane. You will know the airplane is passing through approximately level flight when the needle stops its movement in one direction and begins to move in the opposite direction. Therefore, when you include the airspeed indicator in the scan with the attitude indicator, altimeter, and vertical speed indicator, it gives you positive pitch control information.

BANK CONTROL INSTRUMENTS

Banking the wings of an airplane normally results in a turn. Therefore, in order to fly a given heading, you should attempt to keep the wings of the airplane level with the horizon while maintaining coordinated flight.

ATTITUDE INDICATOR

The principal instrument used for bank control is the attitude indicator. The heading indicator and turn coordinator are used to indicate when a change in bank is required.

HEADING INDICATOR

In coordinated flight, bank attitude also is indicated on the heading indicator. Generally, if the heading displayed on the indicator is not changing, the wings are level. On the other hand, a slow heading change indicates a shallow bank angle, while a rapid change in heading indicates a steep bank.

TURN COORDINATOR

When the miniature airplane in the turn coordinator is in a wings-level position, the airplane is maintaining a constant heading. If the wings of the miniature airplane are displaced from the level flight position, the airplane is turning in the direction that the miniature airplane is banking. [Figure 7-4]

Remember that the ball in the inclinometer indicates whether you are maintaining coordinated flight. If the ball is off center, the airplane is slipping or skidding. When this occurs, make corrections with appropriate coordinated rudder and aileron pressure. [Figure 7-5]

The principal reference for making bank corrections is the attitude indicator. To make a heading change, use a bank angle equal to one-half of the difference between the present heading and the desired heading. However, the angle you use should not exceed that necessary for a standard-rate turn. For example, if your desired heading is 300° and your present heading is 290°, you need to change your heading by 10°. Therefore, you should use a bank angle no greater than one-half of 10° or, in this example, 5° of bank.

To correct a heading deviation, use a bank angle equal to one-half the deviation, but do not exceed the bank required for a standard-rate turn.

CLIMBS

You enter a climb by applying back pressure to the control wheel and using the attitude indicator to establish climb attitude. Once airspeed

Figure 7-4. The turn coordinator indicates the rate of turn. When a wingtip of the miniature airplane is aligned with one of the white marks at the side of the instrument, the airplane is turning at three degrees per second. This is a standard-rate turn.

Figure 7-5. This instrument indicates a slip, since the ball of the inclinometer is off-center in the same direction the miniature airplane is banked. To correct this problem, apply right rudder pressure to center the ball and coordinated aileron pressure to maintain the desired rate of turn.

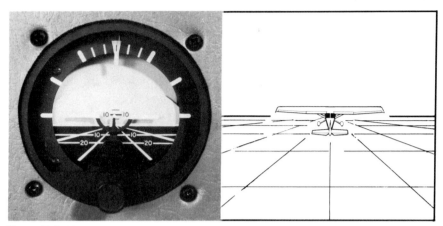

Figure 7-6. To establish a climb from cruising airspeed, raise the nose to about a two-bar width, nose-high pitch attitude. This adjustment is a general guideline and varies with the airplane you use, as well as the rate of climb and the climb airspeed you desire.

has stabilized, use the attitude indicator to further adjust pitch attitude to achieve a desired airspeed. [Figure 7-6]

Use light control pressures to initiate and maintain the climb, since pressures change as the airplane decelerates. You may advance power to the climb power setting at the same time you change pitch, provided you do not exceed maximum r.p.m. limits.

If you have made the transition smoothly, the vertical speed indicator will show an immediate upward trend and will stabilize at a rate appropriate to the stabilized airspeed and pitch attitude. As you make the transition from cruise to climb, use additional right rudder pressure in order to compensate for P-factor and to maintain the desired heading.

During climb entry, maintain directional control by referring to the attitude indicator, heading indicator, and turn coordinator. Once you have established and stabilized the climb, trim away control pressures. If the instrument scan reveals any deviation from the desired heading or pitch attitude, make the required correction by referring to the attitude indicator while continuing the scan. [Figure 7-7]

LEVELOFF FROM CLIMBS

Lead the leveloff by 10% of the vertical speed.

You should initiate the leveloff from a climb before reaching the desired altitude because the airplane continues to climb at a decreasing rate throughout the transition to level flight. An effective guideline is to lead the altitude by 10% of the vertical speed indication. For example, if the airplane is climbing at 500 feet per minute, you should begin the leveloff 50 feet prior to reaching the desired altitude. To level off and accelerate

Figure 7-7. Here are the typical instrument indications of a training airplane in a stabilized, straight climb. The only instrument which changes is the altimeter. All others should remain steady.

to cruise speed, apply smooth, steady, forward elevator pressure. During the transition from climb to cruise, relax right rudder pressure and check the heading indicator to ensure that you maintain the desired heading. As you establish level flight using the attitude indicator, the airspeed increases to cruise speed and the vertical speed needle moves slowly toward zero. At this time, you may make rough trim adjustments. Then, as you reach cruise speed, reduce power to the recommended cruise setting and make final trim adjustments.

DESCENTS

To enter a descent, use the attitude indicator to establish the descent attitude, then reduce the power as required. As the pitch attitude and descent rate stabilize, trim the airplane. For a constant-rate descent, use the vertical speed indicator to tell you when to change pitch. During a constant airspeed descent, you will need to adjust the pitch anytime you deviate from the desired airspeed. You perform constant airspeed descents by using the pitch attitude of the airplane to control airspeed and engine power to control rate of descent. To enter a descent from cruise without a change in airspeed, smoothly reduce the power to the desired setting and reduce the pitch attitude slightly so the airspeed remains constant. The degree of pitch change and power reduction will vary according to the particular airplane used for training. Once the pitch attitude and power are established, you should cross-check the airspeed indicator with the attitude indicator.

When the airplane is descending at cruise airspeed, you control the rate of descent with small power adjustments. However, when a power change is made, you must cross-check the airspeed and attitude indicator to ensure the airspeed remains constant. This is important, because any change you make in power also requires a corresponding change in pitch attitude to maintain a constant airspeed.

LEVELOFF FROM DESCENTS

As in other leveloff procedures, begin leveloff from a descent before you reach the desired altitude; the amount of lead depends on the rate of descent. In a standard 500 f.p.m. rate of descent, the leveloff normally is led by 10% of the descent rate (50 feet). As you reach the leadpoint, slowly add power to the appropriate level flight cruise setting, and smoothly adjust the pitch to a level flight attitude. Frequently, include the attitude indicator in your scan as you level off. After you have stabilized the pitch attitude and airspeed in straight-and-level flight, remove control pressures by trimming.

TURNS

To enter a turn, apply coordinated aileron and rudder pressure in the direction of the turn. Use the attitude indicator to establish the approximate angle of bank required for a standard-rate turn. Additional lift is needed to offset that portion of the vertical component of lift which is diverted in the turn. Therefore, raise the pitch attitude slightly to maintain altitude. As you establish the turn, adjust the nose of the miniature airplane so it is slightly above the level flight position on the horizon bar.

As the turn progresses, check the turn coordinator to determine if you are maintaining a standard-rate turn. If you are not, make a bank adjustment on the attitude indicator. Include the heading indicator in your scan to determine progress toward the desired heading. Furthermore, check the altimeter to determine that a constant altitude is being maintained throughout the turn. [Figure 7-8]

The principal instrument reference for the roll-out is the attitude indicator. Since you have held a slightly nose-high attitude throughout the turn, relax control wheel back pressure to prevent an altitude gain as you return the airplane to straight-and-level flight. As you attain the wings-level position, continue your instrument scan.

A guideline for determining the amount of lead required for roll-out from a turn is to use approximately one-half the angle of bank. For example, if you are making a standard-rate turn at a bank angle of 15°, begin the roll-out approximately eight degrees before you reach the desired heading.

Figure 7-8. These instruments show a level, standard-rate turn to the right. The bank index at the top of the attitude indicator displays the bank angle as 15°. Notice, too, how the nose of the miniature airplane is slightly above the horizon bar.

CLIMBING AND DESCENDING TURNS

To make climbing and descending turns properly, you will need to combine the techniques used in straight climbs and descents with turning techniques. Initially, establish the climb or descent first, then roll into the turn as the pitch attitude stabilizes. However, as proficiency increases, you should establish the climb or descent simultaneously with the turn.

UNUSUAL ATTITUDES AND RECOVERIES

Any airplane attitude you do not normally use is considered to be an unusual or critical attitude. Such an attitude may result from any number of conditions such as turbulence, disorientation, confusion, preoccupation with cabin duties, carelessness in scanning, errors in instrument interpretation, or lack of proficiency in basic airplane control. By the time you realize the need to concentrate on the instruments, the attitude of your airplane may require immediate attention and recovery.

During the more advanced phases of private pilot training, you may be instructed to take your hands and feet off the controls and close your eyes while your instructor puts the airplane in a unusual attitude. As soon as control of the airplane is returned to you, check the attitude indicator to determine pitch and bank. Then, make immediate corrections to return the airplane to straight-and-level flight.

Figure 7-9. Here are the instrument indications of a typical nose-high unusual attitude. The primary objective for recovery from this situation is to prevent a stall. Therefore, you should simultaneously decrease pitch to reduce the angle of attack, increase power, and roll the wings level.

NOSE-HIGH UNUSUAL ATTITUDE

An unusually high attitude displayed on the attitude indicator may be evidence of a nose-high unusual attitude. Before you initiate recovery, check the other instruments to confirm the reliability of the attitude indicator, since it is possible for the airplane to be in a normal flight attitude with an inoperative attitude indicator. The indications of a nose-high unusual attitude are: a nose-high pitch attitude, decreasing airspeed, and a gain in altitude. [Figure 7-9]

NOSE-LOW UNUSUAL ATTITUDE

The indications of a nose-low unusual attitude are: a nose-low pitch attitude, increasing airspeed, rapid loss of altitude, and a high rate of descent. Your primary objective in a nose-low unusual attitude recovery is to avoid an excessively high airspeed or load factor. [Figure 7-10]

Pilots without instrument ratings who continue flight into adverse weather conditions almost always encounter well-developed, power-on spirals resulting from nose-low unusual attitudes. In this situation, they sense the increased speed of the airplane due to the increased slipstream noise and obviously high engine r.p.m. The normal reaction to a nose-down attitude is to apply control wheel back pressure. However, in this instance, back pressure will result in a continually tightening spiral.

Figure 7-10. This airplane is in a nose-low unusual attitude. In this case, you should simultaneously reduce power and roll the wings level. Then, gently raise the nose to the level flight attitude. If you attempt to raise the nose before you roll the wings level, the increased load factor can result in an accelerated stall, a spin, or a force exceeding the airplane design load factor.

CHECKLIST

After studying this section, you should have a basic understanding of:

✓ **Flight instruments** — How to use each of the flight instruments during instrument flight.

✓ **Scanning** — What scanning is, how to use it correctly, and what some of the common scanning problems are.

✓ **Straight-and-level flight** — How straight-and-level flight is maintained solely by reference to instruments, which instruments show deviations in heading and altitude, and how to correct these deviations.

✓ **Climbs and descents** — How to enter, maintain, and level off from climbs and descents by instrument references.

✓ **Turns** — What a standard-rate turn is and how to make a turn at a standard rate to a preselected heading.

✓ **Unusual attitude recoveries** — How to recognize and recover from nose-high and nose-low unusual attitudes.

NIGHT OPERATIONS

In many respects, night flight is easier and more pleasant than daytime flying. Traffic is usually easier to locate at night, and the air is generally smoother and cooler, resulting in more comfortable flight and better airplane performance. Furthermore, at night the pilot experiences less airport traffic pattern congestion and often finds less competition when using communication frequencies. However, because visual acuity is reduced at night, you must consider additional factors and exercise extra caution.

NIGHT FLIGHT CONSIDERATIONS

On a bright, moonlit evening, when the visibility is good and the wind is calm, night flying is not a great deal different than flying during the day. However, you must consider the following factors carefully before making a night flight.

1. Visibility
2. Amount of outside light available
3. Surface winds
4. General weather situation
5. Availability of lighted airports enroute
6. Proper functioning of the airplane and its systems
7. Equipment in the airplane for night flying
8. Your recent night flying experience

PREFLIGHT INSPECTION

Perform the preflight inspection in the usual manner, preferably in a well-lighted area with the aid of a flashlight. Be sure a spare set of fuses is aboard the airplane or, if the airplane is equipped with circuit breakers, check them to see that they are not tripped. A tripped circuit breaker may be an indication of an equipment malfunction, since most circuit breakers cannot be tripped manually. When you discover a tripped circuit breaker during the preflight, reset it and test the associated equipment for proper operation prior to flight.

Check the windshield for dirt that may interfere with vision. Although this is a good preflight procedure anytime, it is especially important before a night flight.

AIRCRAFT LIGHTS

All aircraft operating between sunset and sunrise are required to have operable navigation lights, or **position lights.** You should turn these on during the preflight inspection so you can check them visually to ensure proper operation, then immediately turn them off to avoid excessive drain on the battery. Many airplanes allow you to check for proper operation of the lights from inside the airplane through use of position light detectors. These plastic attachments for the navigation lights convey light above or below the surface of the wing. [Figure 7-11]

All aircraft must have an **anticollision light** system for night operation. A common type is the rotating beacon, which usually is located at the top of the tail and emits red flashes of light. An increasing number of airplanes, however, are being equipped with brilliant, flashing, white strobe lights that can be seen for many miles at night. These lights can also be used in poor visibility conditions during the day. Check the anticollision lighting system during the preflight inspection.

Most airplanes have **landing lights,** and some have **taxi lights** to illuminate the runway and taxiway. These lights may be mounted behind a common lens in the leading edge of the wing or in the cowling. Another installation which usually is restricted to high-performance airplanes is described as a retractable gear-mounted light.

Although you must visually check both the landing light and the taxi light for correct operation during the preflight inspection, do not allow these lights to operate for any length of time with the engine shut down, because of the high electrical drain on the battery. Your preflight check should include inspection for illumination, cracks in the lens, and the correct aiming angle of each light. However, take care when you are operating the landing and taxi lights to avoid shining them in the direction of another aircraft, since this can impair the other pilot's night vision.

All aircraft operated at night are required to display position lights.

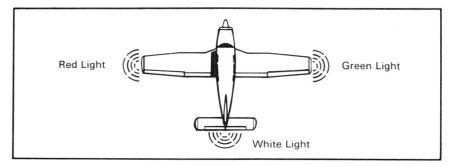

Red Light

Green Light

White Light

Figure 7-11. A red position light is located on the left wingtip, a white light on the tail, and a green light on the right wingtip.

A flashlight is a necessity for any night flight.

All modern airplanes are equipped with a system for lighting the instrument panel and instruments. Prior to any night flight, check the panel lighting system to determine that it is operating satisfactorily. Carry a flashlight on night flights to provide an alternate source of light if interior lights malfunction.

Panel lighting generally is controlled by a rheostat switch which allows you to select the intensity of light that best satisfies your needs. There may be separate rheostats for the flight instruments, engine instruments, and radios. The light intensity should be adjusted just bright enough so you are able to read the instrument indications. If the lighting is too bright, a glare results and your night vision suffers.

Flood lighting is a common method of illuminating the entire instrument panel with one light source. This system uses a single ceiling-mounted light with a rheostat to regulate its intensity. Its beam is directed over both the flight and engine instruments. Flood lighting seems to produce the most glare if the intensity is too high.

Post lighting provides each instrument with its own light source, which is adjacent to the instrument. Each post light beam is directed at the instrument and is shaded from your eyes. Generally, there are two or more rheostats for this lighting system — one for the flight instruments, another for the engine instruments. In addition, there may be controls for illumination of fuel tank selectors, switch panels, radios, and convenience lighting.

Internal instrument lighting is similar to post lighting, except that the light source is located inside the instrument itself. The magnetic compass and radios generally utilize internal lighting. Luminescent lettering is often used with internal lighting to permit instrument interpretation with less light. This type of lighting normally produces the least amount of glare.

CABIN FAMILIARIZATION

As part of the preflight inspection, you should become thoroughly familiar with the airplane's cabin, instrumentation, and control layout. You should practice locating each instrument, control, and switch, both with and without cabin lights. Since some switches and circuit breaker panels may be hard to see at night, be sure that you are able to locate them in poor lighting conditions.

VISUAL IMPRESSIONS

During early training in night flight, you will probably find the initial visual impressions after traffic pattern departure to be strikingly different than those you are accustomed to during daytime flying. Therefore, orientation in the local flying area will help you relate chart information to actual terrain and landmarks under night conditions.

Usually, the outlines of major cities and towns are clearly discernible at night. Major metropolitan areas are visible during favorable weather from distances up to 100 miles or more, depending upon the flight altitude. Major highways tend to stand out at night because of the presence of numerous automobile headlights. Less traveled roads are usually not seen easily at night unless the moonlight is bright enough to reveal them.

On clear, moonlit nights, outlines of the terrain and other surface features are dimly visible. For example, you can often discern the outlines of bodies of water by noting the reflection of the moonlight. However, on extremely dark nights, terrain features are nearly invisible, except in brightly lighted, populated areas.

ENGINE STARTUP

Use caution in the engine startup procedure at night, since it is difficult for other persons to determine that you intend to start the engine. In the daytime you shout, "Clear!" At night, in addition to this, turning on the position lights or momentarily flashing other aircraft lights helps warn others that the propeller is about to rotate.

TAXI TECHNIQUE

After you have started the engine and checked the oil pressure, turn on other necessary electrical equipment, including the rotating beacon. However, the taxi light normally should be left off until you are actually ready to taxi.

Airplane taxi and landing lights usually cast a beam that is narrow and concentrated. Because of this fact, taxi light illumination to the side is minimal and taxi speed should be slower at night, especially in congested ramp areas. Initially, it is more difficult to judge distances, and it takes some adaptation to taxi within the limitations of the area covered by the taxi light.

PRETAKEOFF CHECK

When you stop the airplane at the runup area, turn off the taxi and landing lights until you complete the runup. In addition to the usual checklist procedures, check the radios carefully for operation. During the runup, watch for a drop in the intensity of the lighting equipment when you reduce power to idle. A pronounced drop in intensity may indicate a problem. To check the system, add power and check the ammeter, or loadmeter, for proper indications.

TAKEOFF

You can minimize the differences between day and night flight by scheduling a night checkout which begins at twilight. When you use this procedure, the takeoffs, landings, and traffic pattern work begin in the more familiar daylight environment and, as darkness increases, you make the transition to night operation gradually. This procedure is highly recommended.

As you initiate the takeoff roll, select a reference point down the runway, such as the point where the runway edge lights seem to converge. If you look directly toward the lights near the airplane, you will experience an illusion of speed. However, you can use these lights to keep the airplane properly aligned during the takeoff roll.

Use the attitude indicator for pitch and bank reference after takeoff at night.

During your first night takeoff, you may notice the lack of reliable outside visual references after you are airborne. This is particularly true at small airports located in sparsely populated areas. To compensate for this effect, use the flight instruments in conjunction with available outside visual references. Immediately after liftoff, maintain a normal climb attitude on the attitude indicator. The vertical speed indicator and altimeter also should indicate a climb. Include the airspeed indicator in the cross-check as well. The first 500 feet of altitude gain after takeoff is considered to be the critical period in transitioning from the comparatively well-lighted airport area into what sometimes appears as total darkness.

NIGHT MANEUVERS

In many ways, night flight is similar to flying in marginal VFR conditions. There are times when you need the discipline of an instrument-rated pilot, because your senses may urge you to believe your physical sensations rather than the instrument indications. Your *Private Pilot Manual* covers some of the illusions you may experience at night.

Preparation for night flying should include a review of basic instrument flight techniques. Your instructor may conduct a simulated instrument session which includes straight-and-level flight, turns, climbs, climbing turns, descents, descending turns, and unusual attitude recoveries.

COLLISION AVOIDANCE AT NIGHT

Due to the reduction in outside visual reverences, you may have a tendency to spend too much time looking at the flight instruments. Therefore, you must make a special effort to devote enough time to scan for traffic. You can determine the position of other aircraft at night by scanning for position lights and anticollision lights. As discussed in the *Private Pilot Manual*, the placement of position lights helps you determine another aircraft's direction of flight.

ENROUTE PROCEDURES

High cruising altitudes provide improved margins of safety, especially for night flights. There are several reasons for this. First, range is usually greater at higher altitudes. Second, gliding distance is greater in the event of engine failure. Third, pilotage is less difficult, because you usually can see lighted landmarks at greater distances. The reception range of many navigation aids is also greater.

You should use a subdued white cabin light for reading charts, since considerable information on charts is printed in red and disappears under red cabin lighting. If a map reading light is not available in the airplane, use your flashlight for reading the charts. Place special emphasis on the terrain elevations provided on the charts to ensure adequate obstruction clearance.

WEATHER

When you are operating at night, you must be especially attentive to signs of changing weather conditions. It is extremely easy to fly into an overcast at night, because you cannot detect the clouds easily by direct visual observation. There are several guidelines that will assist you at night if you inadvertently fly into heavy haze, patches of clouds, or an overcast.

It is relatively easy to fly into undetected clouds or fog at night.

If you are approaching an overcast, you can sometimes detect the presence of the clouds because the lights in the distance disappear. In addition, a luminous glow, or halo, around the position lights indicates imminent or actual penetration of IFR weather conditions.

You can get another indirect visual cue by turning on the landing light for a short period of time. On a very clear night, the beam of a landing light is barely scattered by particles in the air. However, if there is considerable haze or the temperature and dewpoint are converging rapidly and cloud formation is imminent, you will notice some scattering of the beam. If actual penetration of a cloud layer occurs, the light beam will be dispersed in all directions. If inadvertent penetration of IFR conditions occurs, you should calmly, but immediately, initiate a 180° standard-rate turn, using the flight instruments to fly out of the weather conditions.

Before you fly at night, obtain a thorough weather briefing. Give special attention to any information in the weather briefing that indicates possible formation of clouds, overcast, fog, or precipitation.

NORMAL LANDINGS AT NIGHT

In some respects, night landings are actually easier than daytime landings, since the air is generally smooth and the disrupting effects of turbulence and excessive crosswinds usually are absent. However, there are a few special considerations and techniques that apply to landings at night.

You should fly the same "standard" approach at night that you use during the day.

Many pilots have a tendency to make higher or lower approaches at night than during the daytime. Therefore, give careful consideration to traffic pattern procedures and to the factors that enable you to maintain the proper glide angle on final approach. Fly a standardized approach pattern using the altimeter and vertical speed indicator to monitor the rate of descent.

The runway lights provide an effective peripheral vision cue for beginning the landing flare. Runway lights, when you see them with peripheral vision, seem to rise and spread laterally as you near the proper touchdown point.

It is standard operating procedure to use your landing lights for night landings, even though they may cause an illusion of runway height. The portion of the runway illuminated by the landing lights seems higher than the dark area surrounding it. This effect tends to cause you to flare high. In addition, focusing your attention on the area immediately in front of the airplane is poor practice, but the arrangement of most landing lights tends to encourage this technique. When using landing lights, your sighting point should be near the forward limit of the lighted area.

Proper preparation for night flight should include landings made both with and without the aid of the landing lights. As previously discussed, the cues for the proper maintenance of the approach profile are derived from the altimeter indications and, when on final, from the perspective created by the size, shape, and patterns of the runway lights. Check the altimeter and the vertical speed indicator against your position in the pattern to monitor the approach.

You can make a no-light landing in the manner described or modify it slightly in the flare and touchdown phases. Hold a normal approach until you are over the threshold where the flare normally begins. At this point, slow the airplane by using a slightly higher-than-normal pitch attitude. This attitude should remain constant until touchdown. With your hand on the throttle, adjust power as needed and lower the plane to the runway by maintaining a very shallow sink rate. Be careful to avoid an increasing sink rate or the approach of a stall.

Good landings without landing lights require practice. After the first few approaches and touchdowns, you will be able to execute them accurately. Familiarity with the technique allows you to make a safe night landing with the landing lights inoperative.

EMERGENCY LANDINGS

If it is necessary for you to make a forced landing at night, use the same procedures as those recommended for daytime emergency landings. If it is available, turn on the landing light during the final approach to assist you in avoiding obstacles in the approach path. Highways may be used as emergency landing strips at night, but you must exercise extreme caution to avoid any powerlines crossing the highway.

Prudent pilots select routes for night flights that keep them within reach of airports as much of the time as possible. For example, a course comprised of a series of 25° zigzags in the direction of various airports is only 10% longer than a straight course. Higher cruising altitudes also are advantageous. At 10,000 feet AGL, a light airplane with a glide ratio of 8 to 1 may glide 13 miles. This distance may place the airplane within range of an airport.

CHECKLIST

After studying this section, you should have a basic understanding of:

✓ **Special considerations** — What the differences are between daylight and night operations and the additional factors that should be considered before starting a flight at night.

✓ **Aircraft lighting** — What lights are required to be displayed on an airplane operated at night and how these lights are used to assist you in collision avoidance.

✓ **Airplane operation** — How the various phases of night flight are conducted from preflight to shutdown.

✓ **Night emergencies** — What some of the procedures are that minimize the hazards of an engine failure or other emergency at night.

EXERCISES

INTRODUCTION

These workbook exercises are designed to complement the *Maneuvers Manual* and the video presentations. Each exercise is correlated with a specific chapter and section; for example, Exercise 1A applies to Chapter 1, Section A of the *Maneuvers Manual*.

The exercises contain multiple choice, true/false, matching, and completion questions. To answer the multiple choice questions, circle the number of the correct choice. Fill in the appropriate blanks to answer the other questions. Further instructions may appear at the beginning of a section or within the body of an individual exercise, when necessary. The answers to all of the exercises are grouped at the back of the manual following the exercises for Chapter 7.

EXERCISE 1

GROUND OPERATIONS

SECTION A
PREFLIGHT AND ENGINE STARTING

1. To ensure that all steps are completed, you should use a _____ _____.

2. In addition to being listed in the required flight manual, airplane _____ are required to be marked or placarded.

3. One aircraft document or certificate that must be available, but not necessarily on board the aircraft, is the

   1. engine logbook.
   2. radio station license.
   3. aircraft registration certificate.
   4. aircraft airworthiness certificate.

4. Because of the possibility of fuel contamination, you should check the fuel _____ (before, after) each flight.

5. Due to the excessive stress that can be caused by nicks in the propeller, they should be repaired by a _____ _____ before flight.

6. Air entering the engine is filtered to remove dust and dirt when the carburetor heat control is in the _____ position.

7. To aid in starting, you should use the primer to pump fuel into the engine _____.

8. _____ (True, False) Before you start the engine, a thorough look around the propeller eliminates the need for opening a window or door and shouting, "Clear!"

9. _____ (True, False) To avoid damage to the starter motor, release the starter as soon as the engine starts.

10. Excessive friction within the engine after starting can be caused by _____ r.p.m. or _____ oil pressure.

11. In warm weather, you should shut down the engine if the oil pressure does not register properly within _____ seconds after starting.

12. After you start an engine in cold weather, the oil pressure should register properly within _____ seconds.

SECTION B
TAXIING, ENGINE SHUTDOWN, AND TIEDOWN

1. During normal operations, it takes more power to _____ (start, keep) the airplane moving than to _____ (start, keep) it moving.

2. Many flight instructors recommend the use of a taxi speed that is no faster than a _____ _____ .

3. While taxiing, you typically use the rudder pedals to move the _____, which causes the airplane to turn.

4. To make a small radius turn, apply the rudder pedal fully in the direction of the turn, then lightly apply the _____ on that pedal.

5. If you are taxiing at five knots into a 20-knot headwind, the total airflow velocity over the wings is

   1. 10 knots.
   2. 15 knots.
   3. 20 knots.
   4. 25 knots.

Answer questions 6 through 9 by matching the correct control position with the appropriate wind condition encountered during taxi.

6. _____ Slight headwind   A. Full left aileron and neutral control wheel

7. _____ Strong tailwind   B. Neutral aileron and control wheel full forward

8. _____ Right quartering tailwind   C. Neutral aileron and control wheel

9. _____ Left quartering headwind   D. Full left aileron and control wheel full forward

10. _____ (True, False) Although it is good practice to use checklists during preflight and engine starting, there is no need to use a checklist for engine shutdown.

11. When moving an airplane by its propeller, you should apply pressure to the propeller blade only near its _____.

12. The control surfaces may be damaged during high winds or gusty conditions if you do not use _____ _____ when you secure the aircraft.

PRIMARY MANEUVERS

SECTION A
STRAIGHT-AND-LEVEL FLIGHT

1. During straight-and-level flight, you should maintain a constant altitude and _____ of flight.

2. Control of the airplane's nose and wing positions in reference to the natural horizon is referred to as _____ _____.

3. The best way to control the airplane's pitch attitude is to

    1. concentrate on the altimeter.
    2. select a reference point on the ground.
    3. select a reference point directly in front of you.
    4. focus on a point over the center of the airplane's nose.

4. _____ (True, False) If you drift off your desired heading or altitude, first return to straight-and-level flight, then adjust your attitude reference points to return to your original heading or altitude.

5. The control surface which adjusts the pitch attitude, or position of the airplane's nose, is the _____, or _____.

6. After establishing the cruise airspeed and power, you can use the airspeed to detect variations in _____ attitude.

7. Trim tab adjustments are made to

    1. change the airspeed.
    2. correct the heading.
    3. change the pitch attitude.
    4. remove control wheel pressure.

8. To trim the airplane properly, set the desired pitch attitude and airspeed, then trim away any _____ _____ necessary to hold that attitude.

9. In the accompanying illustration, turn coordinator _____ shows coordinated flight.

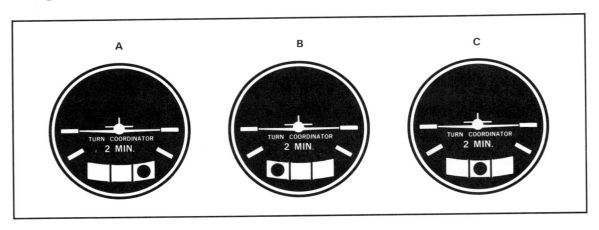

10. Generally, kinesthetic sense is defined as the feel of motion and pressure changes through nerve endings in your organs, muscles, and tendons, and it is sometimes described as the "_____-of-the-_____" sensation.

SECTION B
CLIMBS AND DESCENTS

1. Climbs are practiced to develop your proficiency in establishing the proper climb _____, applying the appropriate _____ pressures, and _____ the airplane correctly.

2. The proper steps for entering a climb from straight-and-level flight are to

   1. add power, increase back pressure to establish the climb attitude, then allow the airspeed to stabilize.
   2. reduce power to attain the desired climb airspeed, then add power and increase back pressure to establish the climb attitude.
   3. increase back pressure to establish the climb attitude and add sufficient power to maintain cruise airspeed.
   4. decrease back pressure to establish the climb attitude and add full power.

3. The left-turning tendencies created by such forces as torque, P-factor, and spiraling slipstream are most pronounced at _____ (high, low) power settings and _____ (high, low) airspeeds.

Match the climb speeds listed in questions 4 through 6 with the letters corresponding to the appropriate descriptions.

4. _____ Cruise climb speed

   A. Greatest altitude gain in shortest distance

5. _____ Best rate-of-climb speed

   B. Greatest altitude gain per minute

6. _____ Best angle-of-climb speed

   C. Best engine cooling and forward visibility

7. If you have a 600 f.p.m. rate of climb, you should begin your leveloff approximately _____ feet below your desired altitude.

8. You practice descents to learn the techniques for losing altitude without gaining excessive _____ and for controlling the rate of descent with power and _____ _____.

9. In many airplanes, the pitch attitude for a descent at approach speeds is nearly the same as the attitude used for _____-_____-_____ flight.

10. During a constant airspeed descent, you control the rate of descent by adjusting
    1. trim.
    2. power.
    3. pitch attitude.
    4. the angle of attack.

11. _____ (True, False) A maximum range descent is performed with full flaps.

SECTION C
TURNS

1. When you initiate a left turn, the left aileron moves _____ (up, down) and the right aileron moves _____ (up, down).

2. _____ (True, False) The steepness of bank in a turn entry depends on how long you hold the ailerons deflected.

3. Increased back pressure is required in turns to increase _____ _____.

4. Adverse yaw is the result of a change in the lift produced by the _____.

5. In a coordinated turn entry, you should simultaneously apply aileron and _____ pressure.

6. If you are in a turning, nose-high attitude with low airspeed and increasing altitude, to return to level flight you need to

    1.   decrease pitch.
    2.   decrease airspeed.
    3.   decrease the bank angle.
    4.   increase the bank angle.

7. To roll out of a turn at a predetermined point, lead the roll-out point by _____-_____ of the bank angle.

8. To make a turn by instrument references, you replace the natural horizon reference with the _____ _____ .

9. A turn rate of three degrees per second is called a _____-_____ turn.

10. As true airspeed increases, the bank angle needed to maintain a standard-rate turn _____ (increases, decreases).

11. If you are making a standard-rate turn, how long will it take you to turn 90°?

    1.   15 seconds
    2.   30 seconds
    3.   1 minute
    4.   3 minutes

SECTION D
TRAFFIC PATTERNS

1. If an airport has a nonstandard traffic pattern, make your turns to the _____ .

2. At uncontrolled airports, you normally enter the traffic pattern abeam the midpoint of the runway at a _____ ° angle to the _____ leg.

3. Traffic pattern altitude is generally _____ feet above ground level.

Use the following illustration to answer questions 4 through 8. Complete the exercise below by placing the correct letter identifying the traffic pattern segments next to the identifying names.

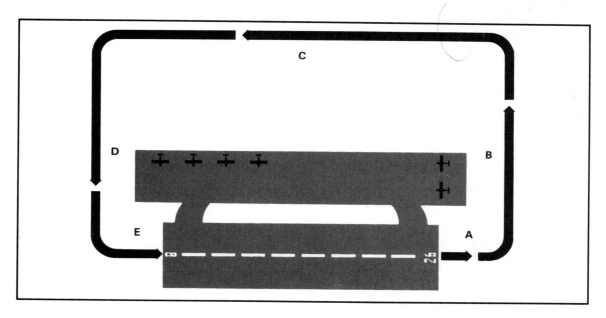

4. _____ Takeoff (upwind) leg

5. _____ Base leg

6. _____ Downwind leg

7. _____ Final approach leg

8. _____ Crosswind leg

9. _____ (True, False) Each leg of the traffic pattern is normally flown at a distance of one-half to one mile away from the runway.

10. At an airport with an operating control tower, you are normally required to have and use a _____-_____ radio.

11. To make your aircraft more clearly visible during the day, turn on the _____ and _____ lights.

EXERCISE 3
TAKEOFFS AND LANDINGS

SECTION A
NORMAL AND CROSSWIND TAKEOFFS

1. The pretakeoff check is important because it helps you verify proper operation of the airplane's _____ and _____.

2. If you notice an abnormal condition during the pretakeoff check, you should
    1. attempt a takeoff.
    2. return the airplane for maintenance.
    3. run the engine at 2,000 r.p.m. to see if the condition improves.
    4. let the engine idle until it is warmed up and try the check again.

3. When you apply carburetor heat during the pretakeoff check, proper operation is indicated by a(n) _____ (increase, decrease) in engine r.p.m.

4. Before taxiing onto the runway, you should check both the approach and departure paths for _____.

5. To maintain directional control during the takeoff roll, you must use
    1. power.
    2. the rudder pedals.
    3. the control wheel.
    4. differential braking.

6. Wind that acts at right angles to the airplane's path on takeoff or landing is called the _____ _____.

7. _____ (True, False) It is common to use full aileron deflection initially on a crosswind takeoff roll until the airplane accelerates and the controls become more effective.

8. Airplanes tend to weathervane because of wind striking the _____ _____ and _____ surfaces.

9. If the engine fails at low altitude just after takeoff, you should make small turns only as necessary to avoid obstacles and land _____ _____.

Using the following wind component chart, answer questions 10 through 13 by filling in the crosswind component under each condition.

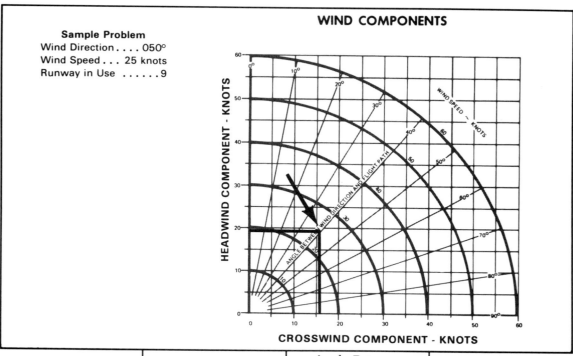

WIND COMPONENTS

Sample Problem
Wind Direction . . . . 050°
Wind Speed . . . 25 knots
Runway in Use 9

Question	Wind Velocity	Angle Between Wind Direction and Runway	Crosswind Component
10.	30 kts.	20°	
11.	20 kts.	70°	
12.	18 kts.	90°	
13.	15 kts.	40°	

SECTION B
NORMAL AND CROSSWIND LANDINGS

1. The angle between the nose of the airplane and the desired path over the ground is called the

   _____ _____ .

2. To prepare for the landing, begin planning on the _____ leg of the traffic pattern.

3. On the downwind leg, the airplane's ground track should be approximately one-half to one mile from, and _____ to, the runway.

4. At the 180° point in the traffic pattern, reduce the _____ and allow the airspeed to slow to _____ speed.

5. The point where you make an initial overall assessment of your approach in terms of altitude, airspeed, distance from the runway, and wind is referred to as the _____ _____.

6. Regardless of the actions taken at any point in the approach, you should continually assess your position and make necessary corrections to arrive accurately at the _____ _____.

7. _____ (True, False) Complete the turn to final at approximately 300 to 400 feet AGL, and plan the roll-out on the extension of the runway centerline.

8. On final approach, as the wind speed increases, your groundspeed _____.

9. The apparent shape of the runway remains fixed if you maintain a constant _____ _____.

10. The approach speed is frequently near the best angle-of-glide speed, which means any other airspeed will result in a _____ (higher, lower) rate of descent.

11. The process of changing the airplane from a glide, or descent attitude, to a landing attitude is called the _____.

12. In most training airplanes, the transition from the descent to a landing attitude begins at approximately _____ to _____ feet above the ground.

13. When executing a go-around, you normally adjust your flight path to the _____ (left, right) so you will not overfly the runway.

14. When compared with a landing using flaps, the rate of descent on a no-flap approach normally is _____ (greater, less) and the approach tends to be _____ (steeper, shallower).

15. _____ (True, False) To execute a go-around, you should add full throttle, accelerate to best angle-of-climb speed, and immediately raise the flaps to the full-up position.

16. On final approach during a crosswind landing, you should lower the wing into the wind and keep the nose pointed straight down the runway through use of opposite _____ pressure.

17. It is normal for the airplane to touch down on one main wheel during a _____ _____.

18. One method used to increase the angle of descent without using flaps or causing an increase in airspeed is known as a _____.

19. During final approach, flaps serve the same purpose as a _____.

20. To compensate for drift during crosswind landings, you normally use a _____ slip.

21. The nose of the airplane remains aligned with the airplane's ground track throughout a _____ slip maneuver.

22. _____ (True, False) During a forward slip in a no-wind condition, the airplane's ground track is a straight line parallel to the longitudinal axis of the airplane.

23. To initiate a forward slip, lower one wing using aileron control and simultaneously apply opposite rudder to keep the airplane from turning in the direction of the _____ (raised, lowered) wing.

24. To prevent the airspeed from increasing when executing a slip, position the nose slightly _____ the normal gliding position.

SECTION C
EMERGENCY LANDING PROCEDURES

1. Number the following steps in the proper sequence for the execution of an emergency landing.

   _____ Use an appropriate emergency checklist to attempt to determine the cause of the power loss, and attempt a restart of the engine.

   _____ Establish the best glide speed.

   _____ Establish a landing approach.

   _____ Turn to a heading that will take the airplane to a field.

   _____ Scan the immediate area for a suitable field.

2. If time permits, declare an emergency on the radio and be sure to provide your _____ as accurately as possible.

3. _____ (True, False) During an emergency landing, you should circle away from the field, then make a long, straight-in glide.

4. The most common cause of engine power loss is inadvertent _____ exhaustion.

5. Ideally, when you reach normal traffic pattern altitude, the airplane should be at the _____° point.

6. When should you use flaps during an emergency landing approach?

    1. On short final
    2. Early in the final approach
    3. As soon as you select a field
    4. As required to reach the selected field

ADVANCED MANEUVERS

SECTION A
FLIGHT AT CRITICALLY SLOW AIRSPEEDS

1. One of the objectives of flight at critically slow airspeeds is to learn the relationships of load factor, pitch attitude, airspeed, and _____ control.

2. Flight at critically slow airspeeds must be sufficiently slow so that immediate indications of a stall will follow any _____ (increase, decrease) in speed or power, or any _____ (increase, decrease) in load factor.

3. The proper technique for reducing airspeed for flight at critically slow airspeeds is to

    1. reduce power and begin a descent.
    2. lower flaps while reducing power.
    3. begin a climb and reduce power to allow airspeed to decay.
    4. reduce power and apply back pressure as required to maintain altitude.

4. When the airplane is slow and you apply power, the resulting left-turning tendency is partially caused by

    1. P-factor.
    2. decreased torque.
    3. the low angle of attack.
    4. the decrease in the spiraling slipstream.

5. During flight at critically slow airspeeds, control effectiveness is _____ (increased, reduced), and it is necessary to use _____ (larger, smaller) control movements than normal.

6. _____ (True, False) The correct procedure for gaining altitude while flying at critically slow airspeeds is to apply full power with no change in pitch attitude.

7. If you retract the flaps suddenly during flight at critically slow airspeeds, you may place the airplane in a(n) _____.

SECTION B
POWER-OFF STALLS

1. _____ (True, False) An objective of practicing stalls is to become familiar with the stall warning and handling characteristics of the airplane as it approaches a stall.

2. During the recovery from a stall, FAR Part 23 specifies that you must be able to prevent more than _____ ° of roll or _____ ° of yaw through normal use of controls.

3. A stall is caused by an excessive angle of attack, which causes the smooth airflow over the upper wing surface to break away, resulting in a loss of _____.

4. An airplane can stall at any _____ and in any flight _____.

5. One indication of an impending stall is
   1. buffeting of the controls.
   2. fluctuating airspeed indications.
   3. loud and intense slipstream noises.
   4. extremely sensitive control pressures.

6. When you initiate the recovery at the first indication of a stall, you are practicing a(n) _____ stall recovery.

7. Secondary stalls are caused by applying _____ (too much, too little) back pressure, which increases the G-loading and _____ (increases, decreases) the stall speed.

8. Your first action in a stall recovery is to _____ (increase, decrease) the angle of attack by releasing back pressure, while simultaneously applying full _____.

9. If you increase the angle of bank, it will _____ (increase, decrease) the stall speed; if you extend flaps, it will _____ (increase, decrease) the stall speed.

SECTION C
POWER-ON AND ACCELERATED STALLS

1. The power-on, straight-ahead stall is the type most frequently encountered shortly after _____.

2. Before entering a power-on stall, you should reduce your airspeed to near _____ speed.

3. As you increase the power and pitch attitude during the power-on stall, you need to use more _____ (left, right) rudder pressure.

4. To recover from a power-on stall, apply full power and simultaneously _____ (increase, decrease) the angle of attack.

5. In a fully developed, power-on stall, pronounced buffeting may occur, and the nose may _____ _____, even though you hold full back pressure.

6. The recommended bank angle for practicing power-on, turning stalls is _____°.

7. _____ (True, False) In an accelerated stall, the term "accelerated" describes the higher-than-normal stall speed which results from an increase in load factor.

8. If you place the airplane in a 60° bank and maintain level flight, you are imposing a load factor of _____ G's.

9. An airplane cannot enter a spin unless it is in a _____ condition.

10. _____ (True, False) Spin recovery technique is always the same for every make or model of airplane.

SECTION D
CONSTANT ALTITUDE TURNS

1. If an entry speed for constant altitude turns is not given in the POH, you should use _____ speed or _____ speed, whichever is slower.

2. If you enter a constant altitude turn too rapidly, you will probably have difficulty establishing the _____ attitude necessary to maintain level flight.

3. You can relieve elevator control pressure during constant altitude turns by using the
   _____.

4. To correct for a loss of altitude during a constant altitude turn, _____
   (increase, decrease) the angle of bank temporarily while _____ (increasing,
   decreasing) the pitch attitude.

5. During constant altitude turns, how many degrees before you reach the desired heading
   should you begin the roll-out?
   1. 10°
   2. 20°
   3. 30°
   4. 40°

6. The overbanking tendency exists because the outside wing of the turn produces
   _____ (more, less) lift than does the inside wing.

7. There is less overbanking tendency in a constant altitude turn to the right because of
   _____ and _____.

GROUND REFERENCE MANEUVERS

1. _____ (True, False) During the execution of ground reference maneuvers, it is necessary for you to divide your attention between the outside and the inside of the airplane.

2. Before beginning any ground reference maneuver, you should estimate the wind's _____ and _____.

3. The rectangular course is similar to the standard _____ _____.

4. The angle of bank in the turning portions of the rectangular course maneuver should not exceed _____°.

5. To achieve symmetrical turns during a rectangular course, you must vary the bank angle according to the
   1. turning radius.
   2. airplane's groundspeed.
   3. airplane's true airspeed.
   4. distance from the field boundary.

6. When the wind is blowing diagonally across a rectangular course, you must use a crab angle on _____ (one, two, four) legs.

7. During S-turns, the shallowest angle of bank occurs just before and just after the airplane crosses the road on a(n) _____ (upwind, downwind) heading.

8. _____ (True, False) Turns around a point should not be flown over populated areas.

9. During turns around a point, the angle of bank at any given position is dependent on the _____ of the circle and the airplane's _____.

10. During the practice of ground reference maneuvers, you normally will limit the airplane's angle of bank to _____°.

EXERCISE 6

MAXIMUM PERFORMANCE TAKEOFFS AND LANDINGS

1. The greatest altitude gain in the shortest distance traveled is provided by the best _____-of-climb airspeed.

2. The greatest altitude gain in a given period of time is provided by the best _____ -of-climb airspeed.

3. The assumed obstructions that you must clear during short-field takeoff practice usually are considered to be _____ feet in height.

4. To execute a short-field takeoff, you must apply back pressure for liftoff as you reach the

    1. cruise-climb airspeed.
    2. best rate-of-climb airspeed.
    3. best angle-of-climb airspeed.
    4. recommended rotation speed.

5. To achieve maximum airplane performance, you should execute short-field landings with the flaps _____ (partially, fully) extended.

6. Compared with a normal approach to landing, the final approach for a short-field landing uses a _____ (steeper, shallower) descent.

7. One of your objectives in the soft-field takeoff is to transfer the weight of the airplane from the main landing gear to the _____ as quickly and smoothly as possible.

8. The soft-field takeoff procedure requires you to accelerate the airplane in a nose-_____ (high, low) attitude, keeping the nosewheel _____ (on, off) the takeoff surface during most of the takeoff run.

9. You actually begin the soft-field takeoff procedure during the _____ (runup, taxi) phase.

10. When an airplane is close to the runway, it may temporarily gain lift from a phenomenon known as _____ _____.

11. Once the airplane is airborne after a soft-field takeoff, you must reduce the pitch attitude gradually to allow the airplane to accelerate to the best _____-of-climb airspeed.

12. _____ (True, False) During a soft-field landing, you should hold the nosewheel clear of the soft runway surface as long as possible to reduce the possibility of an abrupt stop.

EXERCISE 7

ATTITUDE INSTRUMENT AND NIGHT FLYING

SECTION A
ATTITUDE INSTRUMENT FLYING

1. The three fundamental skills you use in all instrument flight maneuvers are instrument scanning or cross check, instrument _____, and airplane _____.

2. The instrument which replaces the natural horizon during instrument flight is the _____ indicator.

3. _____ (True, False) The attitude indicator provides all the information necessary for flight during instrument conditions.

4. The continuous systematic observation of the flight instruments during instrument flight is known as _____ _____, or _____.

5. The natural human inclination to rely heavily on one specific flight instrument results in a problem known as _____.

6. Because of conflicting sensations from the inner ear and postural sense, you must learn to trust the flight _____.

7. The flight instrument that provides a pictorial display of the airplane's overall attitude is the
    1. altimeter.
    2. heading indicator.
    3. attitude indicator.
    4. vertical speed indicator.

8. _____ (True, False) A good tight grip on the control wheel ensures smooth and precise attitude control.

9. Because it indicates the direction of pitch change almost instantaneously, the vertical speed indicator is used to determine altitude _____.

10. The attitude indicator is the principal instrument you use during a turn, while the _____ (heading, airspeed) indicator and turn _____ show you when an adjustment in bank is required.

11. For a constant-rate descent at a specified airspeed, the vertical speed indicator is used to determine when a change in _____ (pitch, power) is required.

12. The percentage of the vertical speed used to determine the normal lead for a leveloff from a climb or descent is

    1. 5%.
    2. 10%.
    3. 15%.
    4. 20%.

13. To recover from a nose-high unusual attitude, you should simultaneously decrease _____ to reduce angle of attack, _____ (increase, decrease) power, and roll the wings level.

14. Your immediate concern during the recovery from a nose-low unusual attitude is to

    1. level the wings.
    2. avoid excessive airspeed.
    3. extend the flaps, if retracted.
    4. prevent the bank angle from exceeding 60°.

SECTION B
NIGHT FLYING

1. A night preflight inspection should be performed in a well-lighted area with the aid of a _____.

2. A red position light is located on the _____ wing, a _____ position light on the tail, and a green position light on the _____ wing.

3. _____ (True, False) You should not check taxi and landing lights during preflight, because of the high energy drain on the battery.

4. To provide an alternate source of light if the interior lights malfunction, you should carry a _____ during night flights.

5. In addition to calling, "Clear!" to warn others the propeller is about to rotate, you can turn on the _____ _____ or momentarily flash the _____ _____.

6. If the intensity of lighting equipment drops when you reduce engine r.p.m., you should add power and check the _____, or _____, for proper indications.

7. After the airplane is airborne, it may become necessary to use the flight instruments if the normal _____ references disappear.

8. _____ (True, False) Except in an emergency, you should never attempt a night landing without the landing light illuminated.

ANSWERS

ANSWERS

A

GROUND OPERATIONS

SECTION 1A

1. written checklist
2. limitations
3. 1
4. before
5. certified mechanic
6. COLD (off)
7. cylinders
8. False
9. True
10. high, low
11. 30
12. 60

SECTION 1B

1. start, keep
2. brisk walk
3. nosewheel
4. brake
5. 4
6. C
7. B
8. D
9. A
10. False
11. hub
12. control locks

2 PRIMARY MANEUVERS

SECTION 2A

1. direction
2. attitude flying
3. 3
4. True
5. elevator, stabilator
6. pitch
7. 4
8. control pressure
9. C
10. seat, pants

SECTION 2B

1. attitude, control, trimming
2. 1
3. high, low
4. C
5. B
6. A
7. 60

8. airspeed, pitch attitude
9. straight-and-level
10. 2
11. False

SECTION 2C

1. up, down
2. True
3. total lift
4. ailerons
5. rudder
6. 1
7. one-half
8. attitude indicator
9. standard-rate
10. increases
11. 2

SECTION 2D

1. right
2. 45, downwind
3. 1,000
4. A
5. D
6. C
7. E
8. B
9. False
10. two-way
11. anticollision, landing

TAKEOFFS AND LANDINGS

3

SECTION 3A

1. equipment, systems
2. 2
3. decrease
4. traffic
5. 2
6. crosswind component
7. True
8. vertical stabilizer, rudder
9. straight ahead
10. 10
11. 19
12. 18
13. 10

SECTION 3B

1. crab angle
2. downwind

3. parallel
4. power, approach
5. key position
6. touchdown point
7. True
8. decreases
9. approach angle
10. higher
11. flare
12. 10, 15
13. right
14. less, shallower
15. False
16. rudder
17. crosswind landing
18. slip
19. slip
20. side
21. side
22. False

23. lowered
24. above

SECTION 3C

1. 4
   1
   5
   3
   2
2. position
3. False
4. fuel
5. 180
6. 1

ADVANCED MANEUVERS

4

SECTION 4A

1. altitude
2. decrease, increase
3. 4
4. 1
5. reduced, larger
6. False
7. stall

SECTION 4B

1. True
2. 15, 15
3. lift

4. airspeed, attitude
5. 1
6. imminent
7. too much, increases
8. decrease, power
9. increase, decrease

SECTION 4C

1. takeoff
2. liftoff
3. right
4. decrease
5. pitch down
6. 20

7. True
8. 2
9. stalled
10. False

SECTION 4D

1. cruise, maneuvering
2. pitch
3. trim
4. decrease, increasing
5. 2
6. more
7. torque, P-factor

GROUND REFERENCE MANEUVERS

1. True
2. speed, direction
3. traffic pattern
4. 45

5. 2
6. four
7. upwind
8. True

9. radius, groundspeed
10. 45

 MAXIMUM PERFORMANCE TAKEOFFS AND LANDINGS

1. angle
2. rate
3. 50
4. 4

5. fully
6. steeper
7. wings
8. high, off

9. taxi
10. ground effect
11. angle
12. True

 ATTITUDE INSTRUMENT AND NIGHT FLYING

SECTION 7A

1. interpretation, control
2. attitude
3. False
4. cross checking, scanning
5. fixation
6. instruments
7. 3
8. False
9. trend

10. heading, coordinator
11. power
12. 2
13. pitch, increase
14. 2

SECTION 7B

1. flashlight
2. left, white, right

3. False
4. flashlight
5. position lights, landing light
6. ammeter, loadmeter
7. visual
8. False

INDEX